Native Sons

J. B. Lippincott Company
Philadelphia and New York

Edward Margolies

Native Sons

A Critical Study of Twentieth-Century Negro American Authors

W. E. B. Du Bois	William Attaway
Charles Waddell Chesnutt	Richard Wright
James Weldon Johnson	Chester Himes
Paul Laurence Dunbar	James Baldwin
Langston Hughes	Ralph Ellison
Jean Toomer	Malcolm X
Claude McKay	William Demby
Countee Cullen	LeRoi Jones

Acknowledgments

Although all literary judgments are my own, I should like to thank my wife for her patience, her counsel and invaluable editorial assistance. In addition I should like to express gratitude to the following publishers and individuals for permission to quote from the works cited below.

Arna Bontemps: "Tired," by Fenton Johnson.

Frank Marshall Davis: "Snapshots of the Cotton South."

Doubleday & Company, Inc.: *Blood on the Forge,* by William Attaway. Copyright 1941 by Doubleday & Company, Inc. Reprinted by permission of the publisher.

Grove Press, Inc.: *The Autobiography of Malcolm X.* Reprinted by permission of Grove Press, Inc. Copyright © 1964 by Alex Haley and Malcolm X. Copyright © 1965 by Alex Haley and Betty Shabazz.

   The Dead Lecturer: Poems by LeRoi Jones. Reprinted by permission of Grove Press, Inc. Copyright © 1964 by LeRoi Jones.

Harper & Row, Publishers, Inc.: "Heritage" and "The Shroud of Color" from *Color* by Countee Cullen.

Alfred A. Knopf, Inc.: "The Negro Speaks of Rivers." Copyright 1926 by Alfred A. Knopf, Inc. and renewed 1954 by Langston Hughes. Reprinted from *Selected Poems* by Langston Hughes by permission of the publisher.

   "Young Gal's Blues." Copyright 1942 by Alfred A. Knopf, Inc. Reprinted from *Shakespeare in Harlem* by Langston Hughes by permission of the publisher.

Random House, Inc.: *The Catacombs,* by William Demby. Copyright 1965 by William Demby.

   The Invisible Man, by Ralph Ellison. Copyright 1947, 1948, 1952, by Ralph Ellison.

Totem Press in association with Corinth Books: *Preface to a Twenty Volume Suicide Note,* by LeRoi Jones. Copyright © 1961 by LeRoi Jones.

Twayne Publishers, Inc.: "The Lynching" by Claude McKay.

In Memory of My Father

Contents

Native Sons

Chapter I

Perspectives

In the past thirty years there has arisen a body of writing by American Negro authors which not only possesses considerable artistic merit, but mercilessly exposes the direction in which the "unassimilated" Negro subculture appears to be moving. The picture is not pretty, nor is the outlook necessarily optimistic, for the revolution in Negro attitudes which has produced this literature has not yet found an adequate response in the nation at large, despite the recent spate of civil rights legislation and other ameliorative measures intended to pacify the poor. Ultimately, what is at stake is the future course of American civilization, for unless there is greater alignment of views between white and

Negro Americans, there is bound to be more of the violent civil disorder the country has witnessed in recent years.

The twentieth-century authors considered in this study will be treated largely from the standpoint of their art. Yet it would be well to bear in mind that aesthetics and history are not unrelated. Aesthetics, after all, implies a clarity of expression, a structuring of meaning out of the vast welter of human experience. Insofar as the artist is capable of forcing to the surface the underlying conditions of his life, he is capable of acting to modify these conditions. And insofar as the artist is a touchstone of his civilization, mirroring in his works the experiences of those who share his world, the evolution of his expression is significantly more than a matter of passing interest. If the Negro artist is becoming more articulate, his works more "aesthetic," the historical implications of this development are portentous, dramatic, and challenging.

In one sense, of course, the works of Negro writers are more inherently "American" than those of their white counterparts, just as the Negro is himself more a product of the American environment than most others. For one thing, he was among the first Americans—African slaves were brought to Virginia shores as early as 1619—and thus from the beginning he tasted and imbued and indeed profoundly influenced the changing patterns of American life. Moreover, unlike later immigrants, he carried few of the trappings of his native civilization with him. The new slaves were systematically stripped of tribal and familial ties by plantation owners who feared that any semblance of cultural continuity might lead to future conspiracies and uprisings. As a result, the recently arrived Africans found themselves isolated and alone, not only unable to speak the language of their masters, but often unable to speak to one another as well. Their offspring, as a matter of necessity, learned to communicate in the only common language available to them—English. This swift and brutal severance of all interpersonal and cultural relationships had an unimaginably destructive impact on the African's personality, and the deleterious results of this deindividualization—extended and aggravated by three hundred years of slavery and oppression—remain today as a burning scar on the personality formation of most Negro Americans.

Yet the Negro *has* managed to survive, mainly by reconstructing his psychology around the system of values he discovered in his new country. Undoubtedly he is the only American who has had to rely so exclusively on the American environment in order to recreate his identity. This almost unadulterated Americanness of the Negro is, of course, reflected in his literature—the Negro author in his quest for expression stands as an intensified image of the total American search for self. Alienation, terror and violence have been his premises, as they have been for other American writers from Poe to Norman Mailer. The Negro author, too, has found his environment self-contradictory, ambiguous, and hostile.

But white American authors in their search for identity could look backward into history (Hawthorne, Twain, John Barth), outward to Europe and the Orient (Melville, James, Eliot, Alan Ginsberg), or inward into themselves (Emerson, Dickinson, Fitzgerald, Bellow). Most Negro authors until recently have been unable to give appropriate artistic expression to their understanding, for the Negro subculture has failed to provide such alternative perspectives.

The reasons become apparent when one considers the underlying conditions peculiar to the Negro subculture. Since the Negro is the only American who did not come to America of his own volition, it follows that the political, social, and psychological motivations that impelled other immigrants were not his to begin with. Nor could his descendants recognize or take pride in their African ancestry. Their overwhelming immersion in the American environment tended to reinforce in them feelings of shame and revulsion about their African past—Africa, in the

American *mythos*, has always been pictured as a land of ignorant, pagan savages indifferent or hostile to the enlightened ways of the West. Hence the Negro has always been the most estranged and alienated of Americans. White Americans have at least had their European institutions, values, and traditions to cling to, or modify, or rebel against. The Negro could only model his culture after the white-master civilization that surrounded him. He could not reach back into time or history to seek his roots. History and time were an abyss, a dark and fruitless void. He could not, for the same reasons, reach out to Africa as some white writers sought out Europe. Least of all could he, like white American metaphysical authors, honestly probe his heart—the violence and destruction he might view there would surely destroy him, since as a Negro he was expected to play out a docile, abject role. In short, the modes in which other American writers could describe their understanding have been inaccessible to the Negro from the very start of his history.

Of course, it was all that Negro authors—and other Negro intellectuals as well, for that matter—could do to survive. Their energies were bent for the most part on proving they were as good as, and equal to, other Americans. Their nineteenth- and early twentieth-century letters are surfeited with pleas for the recognition of their own humanity and with protests against their subjugation. The poetry and polemics of free Negroes prior to the Civil War appealed to Americans on humanitarian grounds, on Christian and democratic principles. Even in those parts of the country where slavery did not exist, Negroes, then as now, were subject to the worst forms of political, social, and educational segregation, as well as grinding poverty, police and mob brutality, and all the other evils of the American caste system. Negro authors had neither the time nor the inclination nor the opportunity to treat the great American existential themes of despair, isolation, and violence—although they frequently lived these themes more bitterly than the white authors who wrote about them.

Perhaps the chief tragedy of the Negro subculture has been the effort of Negro middle-class artists to achieve some kind of status for themselves *within* caste limitations, rather than assume more revolutionary attitudes. The few Negro artists who have attained middle-class status have too often elected to ape the finesse and gentility of "white" arts—to seek a better place within the caste system rather than question or attack the system itself.

In this they have had the sanction of an old Negro middle-class tradition. Prior to the Civil War much of the "black bourgeoisie," North and South, was composed of persons of mixed blood sired by white slave owners. Rather than abandon their illegitimate offspring to the uncertainties of plantation labor, the white masters educated them—often in their own homes—and later set them free with enough money to establish themselves. The freed Negroes and their descendants thereupon adopted the manners, morals, and standards of the whites. Frequently they boasted of their infusions of Caucasian blood, and a light complexion became a desirable status symbol. By and large they maintained their advanced standing in the Negro community until long after World War I.

The works of the few writers and intellectuals who sprang from this class mirrored its provincial attitudes and anxieties. They practically all protested not the injustice of racism—which they implicitly accepted—but rather the injustice of assuming that *all* Negroes, regardless of the proportion of white blood that flowed through their veins, were of one despised sort. They debated the moral and psychological issues involved in "passing" and pleaded the tragedies of "mixed bloods" who stood outside and between the white and Negro communities. They excoriated "foreigners," immigrants, and other minority groups who were not as good Americans as they. They extolled the bourgeois virtues—frugality, churchgoing, moderation, gentility, education—and scorned the "low" Negro peasants, vagabonds, and working classes who made life difficult for them. Sometimes they tried to conceal, or at best not to reveal, that they themselves were Negro. To please the white readers who composed most of their audience, they wrote sentimental pieces about ante-bellum plantation days when Negroes were happy, carefree, irresponsible, and devoted to "ol' massa." They wrote dialect poems and generally groveled and grinned in print in the accepted Topsylike manner. Seldom did they achieve anything of enduring value, so obsessed were they with race. And yet despite their contrived superficialities, one may detect in their works feelings of rage, shame, and self-hate. And who could blame them?

There were, to be sure, a few writers in the early part of the new century whose craft and imagination foreshadowed better things to come. I shall discuss several of them in the following chapter, laying stress on the outstanding literary and psychological aspects of their works in the light of the shifting social and historical backgrounds against which they wrote. But the main body of the book will be devoted to individual authors who have seriously engaged the Negro imagination since 1940.

I have made no attempt to write a complete history of Negro letters. Some fine studies have been made along these lines, and a bibliography of them may be found at the back of this volume. Undoubtedly some readers will feel that I have omitted significant works and accorded others disproportionate emphasis. One can, of course, always plead the obvious: individual judgments vary. But one can hope for even greater tolerance if some of the criteria of selection are made clear.

The central concern of this book is the Negro's evaluation of his historical and cultural experience in this century: the Southern community, the continuing migration to the cities, the urban proletariat, miscegenation and interracial love, the Negro church, the expatriate point of view, the new nationalism, and so on. Since these experiences are of a particularly dense and complicated nature, the main focus of this study will rest on the novel, which by virtue of its own peculiar kind of elasticity best accommodates the general categories of subject matter to be discussed. Ancillary literary forms—the drama, the short story, poetry, the essay—will not be overlooked if an important author has employed these in a lifetime of work. And in at least one instance, that of Malcolm X, an autobiography will be cited as material especially relevant to an understanding of the Negro's sensibility. The authors have been selected on generally aesthetic grounds, or for the degree of their influence. In a few cases, however, a lesser-known writer projects a rare or unusual point of view, which may be amplified or pursued by future generations of writers. These have also been treated here.

A word or two about the title of this book, which makes obvious allusion to Richard Wright's famous first published novel, *Native Son* (1940). *Native Son* was a milestone in Negro letters for a variety of reasons, but mainly because it expressed overtly, for the first time, the shame, the terror, the rage, and the self-hatred many Negroes experience in the course of their American lives. Of course, being a Negro American means much more as well—as James Baldwin and Ralph Ellison have been quick to point out—but the dreadful things the artist fears to say about himself are often the very things which need to be said first before he can convey the wealth and variety of his experience. The example of *Native Son* enabled others to deal with a body of subject matter they had hitherto warily skirted. Wright opened up for Negro writers not only the bitterness of their own lives, but other taboo matters as well—miscegenation, homosexuality, the white-Negro power structure, and even the singular freedom a Negro feels in a society that denies him any recognition of his humanity. The courage to "tell it the way it is" is the prime requisite of artistic integrity. Human revelation is the business of the artist; he must write about what he *knows* to be true—imaginatively or otherwise—and the first truths he must know are about himself. *Native Son* provided many Negro authors with these precedents. In its way it liberated them as no other book has done since.

In another way Richard Wright symbolized in his life and work the themes which would concern a whole new generation of Negro writers. As a boy he experienced the terror and oppression of the rural South; his young manhood was spent in Northern cities where he learned the silent, embittered nationalism of black people, their hope and their despair; his last years were passed in Europe, where, denationalized, he supported the cause of worldwide racial equality. Ultimately, however, he stood alone—neither American, nor European, nor African—committed to principles whose realization still appears absurdly unattainable. This book is not the first to owe its inspiration to Richard Wright—nor, one fancies, will it be the last.

Chapter II
The First Forty Years: 1900-1940

One of the most significant figures in Negro life in the twentieth century is William E. Burghardt Du Bois. His collection of essays, *The Souls of Black Folk* (1903), remains today a revolutionary contribution both to Negro letters and to Negro history. The young, Harvard-educated radical—at odds with the accommodationist Negro spokesman, Booker T. Washington—called for full political, social, and economic equality for Negroes just at the time when caste barriers were being erected practically everywhere in the South. His militancy eventually resulted in the establishment of the National Association for the Advancement of Colored People (1911), which he himself headed until the early 1920's.

But perhaps more important than his political activities was Du Bois's eloquent exposition of how it felt to be a Negro—the tensions and the inner conflicts.

> The Negro is a sort of seventh son, born with a veil, and gifted with second-sight in this American world,—a world which yields him no true self-consciousness, but only lets him see himself through the revelation of the other world. It is a peculiar sensation, this double-consciousness, this sense of always looking at one's self through the eyes of others, of measuring one's soul by the tape of a world that looks on in amused contempt and pity. One ever feels his two-ness,—an American, a Negro; two souls, two thoughts, two unreconciled strivings; two warring ideals in one dark body, whose dogged strength alone keeps it from being torn asunder.

Not until Richard Wright's *Native Son,* some thirty-seven years after the publication of Du Bois's book, would the Negro find so moving a spokesman for his spiritual torment.

Du Bois's considerable reputation rests justifiably on his scholarly and political occupations, yet it is in his relatively circumscribed literary output that one perhaps discovers the best insights into his thinking. Besides a number of protest poems—sprinkled liberally with classical and Biblical allusions—Du Bois wrote five novels in his lifetime. The latter three, an historical trilogy published in the late fifties, will not concern us here.

His first novel, *The Quest of the Silver Fleece* (1911), relates the story of two Negro sharecroppers, Bles and Zora, who in the course of a rambling, improbable narrative learn the connection between plantation capitalism and racial oppression. Two such Negro peasants could only exist in the imagination of a detached intellectual theoretician like Du Bois. Their humanity and their speech are unrecognizable—and Du Bois's prose style is an atrocity. It is interesting to note that Du Bois makes Zora, the heroine, acceptable only after she divests herself of her primitive "natural" qualities and embraces a

Northern education. Du Bois evidently found the folk-peasant mentality of the Southern Negro repellent. Indeed, in his later years, when he served as editor of *The Crisis*, an NAACP periodical, he attacked the Harlem Renaissance literature of the 1920's on grounds that its celebration of Harlem low life represented vulgar carica-ture unsuitable for the tastes of respectable readers.

Du Bois's second novel, *Dark Princess* (1928), deals with a future world-wide organization of colored people designed to effect a racial revolution. (Du Bois's own NAACP and the Pan African Congresses he established in the twenties and thirties correspond roughly to the organization he describes in the novel.) In *Dark Princess* Du Bois scarcely manages to relate the experiences of the oppressed firsthand, although his hero, a disillusioned medical student, works for a while as a Pullman porter. In the main, most of his characters are college-educated intellectuals, shady politicians, and aristocrats of one sort or another whose connection with the untutored masses is at best one step removed.

As he explained in *The Souls of Black Folk*, Du Bois regarded the Negro masses as being hopelessly incapable of improving their status without the help of an intel-lectual elite, the "Talented Tenth," comprised of Negro university graduates who could direct the vast majority of the poor and distressed to heights unknown. It is para-doxical, though perhaps not surprising, that several of the most radical supporters of the Negro proletariat—Du Bois, Paul Robeson, Ben Davis, and others—had in their lifetimes very little contact with the poor whom they pre-sumed to represent. Du Bois himself spent a good number of his later years in Europe, occupied more and more with African affairs. He died in Ghana after renouncing his American citizenship. One of his closest associates at the time of his death was Kwame Nkrumah, the Marxist premier, who, like Du Bois, was university-educated and had passed a good portion of his life among self-exiled intellectuals in Europe.

One of the most prolific Negro writers at the turn of the century was Charles Waddell Chesnutt. Chesnutt, born in Cleveland, the son of prosperous parents, spent most of his youth in North Carolina, where he taught school. When he was twenty-two he returned to Ohio, attended college, worked as a court stenographer, and later practiced law. Descended from free Negroes of North Carolina, Chesnutt was apparently so light-complexioned that he could easily have "passed." He chose instead to remain a Negro, but all three of his novels, *The House Behind the Cedars* (1900), *The Marrow of Tradition* (1901), and *The Colonel's Dream* (1905)—melodramatic, propagandistic, and overwritten—deal with the problems of crossing the color barrier. Chesnutt wrote that nearly all his works "with the exception of *The Conjure Woman* have dealt with the problems of mixed blood which, while in the main the same as those of the true Negro, are in some instances and in some respects much more complex and difficult of treatment."

Perhaps Chesnutt's chief distinction is not, as has sometimes been pointed out, that he was the first Negro to employ the short-story form with a modicum of popular success (the stories are on a level not much higher than his novels), but that he was the first Negro to tap the rich vein of Negro folk culture. The popularization of Negro folklore began with Joel Chandler Harris's publication of the Uncle Remus tales in 1879, and in a sense Chesnutt was following a safe literary treadmill. Yet Harris's stories, for all their charm and accuracy of dialect, were intended as nothing more than amusement. Where Harris failed to see the lurking allegory in Br'er Rabbit's attempts to outwit Br'er Fox, Chesnutt did not make that same mistake in the stories he wrote.

His first piece, "The Goophered Grapevine" (1887), is an account of a white man's first meeting with a crafty ex-slave, Uncle Julius. Uncle Julius tells the white author (for a time Chesnutt's publishers concealed from the public that Chesnutt was a Negro) a fantastic story of ante-bellum days, the intent of which is to save a grapevine the author wants to cut down. In 1899 Chesnutt collected seven of these stories in book form under the title *The Conjure Woman*. The stories differ from Harris's in several important respects. The first is that Uncle Julius tells his stories in order to gain some kind of advantage over his white patron. Hence, Uncle Julius emerges as something more than a quaint, lovable minstrel figure. The second is that the stories put the lie to the fast-emerging stereotype of the contented ante-bellum slave. Several of the stories hint darkly at the suffering and cruelties the slaves endured under malevolent masters. The third is that Chesnutt employed folk material and dialect to create original stories, whereas Harris's tales are authentic folk fables related to him by Negroes he had befriended.

After *The Conjure Woman*, Chesnutt forsook the folk tale for the novel. Although he lived until 1932, Chesnutt wrote very little after 1905. The public was not yet ready to accept a Negro author.

By far the best novel produced by a Negro prior to the 1920's was James Weldon Johnson's *The Autobiography of an Ex-Coloured Man* (1912). The work was published anonymously, and it was not until 1927 that the author's name was made public. So convincing was Johnson's voice that *Autobiography* was generally assumed to be an authentic account of a Negro who "passed." Yet in retrospect the novel conforms in many ways to the fictional pattern of the period. The protagonist is so light-skinned (his father comes from an aristocratic white family in the South) that neither he nor his school-mates know he is a Negro until his teacher callously informs him. He is sensitive, talented, and refined; at the age of fourteen he plays Beethoven's "Pathétique" with consummate skill. He deplores the lower element of Negro, whose bad reputation curses the entire race, and carries on lengthy dialectics with his white patron (Negro fiction is replete with this kind of pedan-

try) about race relations and the injustices suffered by
Negroes. And Johnson swerves off the main course of his
narrative to inform the reader, from time to time, about
"picturesque" aspects of Negro life.

The principal strength of the novel lies in Johnson's
occasional lyric style and the thematic unity he gives to
the episodic structure of the book. The main character,
sympathetic but poignantly cowardly, shies away from
making the decisions that would give substance to his life.
His earliest aspirations of becoming a famous colored
musician are ultimately given pathetic reverberations
when, toward the end of the novel, he opts to pass as a
white business man. Yet his weaknesses are shown to
stem chiefly from his own character and not essentially
from the society that terrifies him.

What gives the novel added interest is its panoramic
view of Negro life. The novel opens in pastoral Georgia as
the protagonist prepares to depart by train for the North.
His youth is passed in moderate comfort in a small bi-
racial Connecticut town. The scene then shifts to Atlanta,
where he is about to attend a Negro college, and later to
Jacksonville, where he is forced to associate with migrant
workers in a tobacco plant. From Jacksonville he moves
to New York, and here Johnson describes some of the
criminal, bohemian, and honky-tonk elements of Negro
urban life. (Johnson's settings of Northern Negro life,
especially New York, are among the first by a Negro
novelist and anticipate the Harlem Renaissance school of
writers by about twelve years.) For a time the hero experiences a brief respite in Europe with a wealthy white
patron; then he returns to the rural South to gather folk
material for the music he is hoping to publish. But after
witnessing a lynching he returns North, defeated and purposeless.

Johnson's real life was considerably different. He was
born in 1871, the son of a Virginia freedman and a West
Indian mother, and attended Atlanta and Columbia universities. He first practised law in Florida, but by the turn

of the century he was writing songs for the Negro musical theater, acquiring some reputation as a poet and composer. He served for a while as a consul in Venezuela, and from 1916 to 1930 occupied high administrative posts for the NAACP. During these later years Johnson's literary output was prodigious. In addition to producing volumes of his own verse and editing anthologies of Negro poetry and spirituals, he published a history of the New York Negro, *Black Manhattan* (1930). Three years later he produced his true autobiography, *Along This Way*, partially as an effort to prove to unbelievers that the novel he had written in 1912 was really fiction.

Second to *Autobiography*, Johnson's best literary effort is *God's Trombones* (1927), a number of extended verse sermons somewhat in the manner of a Southern preacher. Here Johnson eschews dialect as smacking too much of the minstrel tradition, and endeavors to reproduce the essences of folk rhythm and imagery. Although he does not altogether fail, the whole thing gives off a faint antiseptic odor, as if Johnson had run his folk material through a sieve to remove its coarser elements, in deference to the refined sensibilities of his readers.

In 1938 Johnson was killed in an automobile accident in Nashville. He had been teaching literature for the past eight years at Fisk University.

The best-known Negro writer of the first part of the century was the poet, Paul Laurence Dunbar. Born in Dayton, Ohio, the son of a fugitive slave who had fought in the Union Army, Dunbar won high academic honors in an all-white high school. But because he was "very black" Dunbar could only find work as an elevator operator.

White friends helped him publish privately his first volume of poetry (*Oak and Ivy*, 1893), but his second collection (*Majors and Minors*, 1895) enjoyed greater notoriety as a result of a favorable review by William Dean Howells. Howells then wrote an introduction to Dunbar's *Lyrics of Lowly Life*, 1896, which established his popularity. In the following nine years, Dunbar published three additional collections (*Lyrics of the Hearthside*, 1899; *Lyrics of Love and Laughter*, 1903; and *Lyrics of Sunshine and Shadows*, 1905).

But despite his success Dunbar was not a happy man. He brooded about his black skin and complained that it marred his love life. His marriage to a poetess does not appear to have lessened his anxieties. He drank copiously, suffered from tuberculosis, and drove himself constantly to avoid debt. Shortly after a lecture tour in New York in 1906, he returned to his home in Denver to die. He was thirty-four years old.

Dunbar's poetry is divided into two broad categories: dialect verse embracing the manners and mores of plantation slaves and the contemporary life of Negro peasants, and poems of a more conventional nature harkening back to the sentimentalities of second-rate late nineteenth-century poets.

Dunbar is not remembered today—nor was he celebrated in his own time—for his nonracial verse, though certainly it was no worse than the standard stuff of his day. His diction is literary and antiquated, and his pious and melancholy themes are too primly boxed in tired, traditional prosody. Oddly, though, Dunbar regarded these as his best poems—they surely comprised the majority of his output—and complained once to James Weldon Johnson that dialect was the "only way to get [white] people to listen to me." Dunbar was in effect saying that folk material did not quite make for respectable literature—an attitude, as we have seen, not uncommon among Negro writers of his period. But there can be little doubt that Dunbar's dialect poetry is superior to his other verse. His ear was excellent—as most phoneticists agree—and he displayed a technical proficiency beyond even that of the Hoosier poet, James Whitcomb Riley, from whom he derived his inspiration.

What must have hurt Dunbar most—whether he realized it or not—was the warm reception he received from white critics like Howells, who readily accepted the painful stereotypes of the dialect verse. No white racist has ever caricatured Negro folk more grossly than Dunbar. His slaves are docile children, contented in the humble service of their white masters. His Negro peasants chase possum, munch watermelon, and generally celebrate life in high animal spirits. Seldom is there any hint of defeat or suffering in their lives. The worst sorrow they undergo is unrequited love—and even this is so smeared with black cork that the reader can rest assured some other simple joy will come along to erase the pain. The best that can be said of Dunbar in this respect is that he treats his Negroes sympathetically—like a benevolent Bourbon sipping juleps on the veranda.

That Howells and other critics enjoyed Dunbar's verse could not have been due solely to Dunbar's facility with sounds and rhythms. Although Howells denied it, he undoubtedly felt, in his humanitarian socialist fashion, that he was doing the Negro a good turn in patronizing Dunbar—just as many white and Negro critics today overpraise works by Negro authors in the benighted belief that they are somehow thereby serving the cause of civil rights. Howells, the supporter of Henry James and Mark Twain in the early stages of their careers, had inherently better judgment. But perhaps even more pertinent was Howells's unconsciously paternalistic view of the Negro. In his preface to *Lyrics of Lowly Life,* Howells lauds Dunbar for tenderly representing the simplicities and limitations of the Negro psychology. Inasmuch as Dunbar was a Negro of "unmixed blood," how then could anyone take his profounder stuff more seriously?

Dunbar's fiction deserves brief comment. His short stories at their best are prose replicas of his dialect poems —at their worst, oversentimentalized versions of the saccharine school of ante-bellum apologists for the South. His novels are badly written, frequently melodramatic and dearily drawn out. Their chief interest lies in the light they throw on Dunbar's social views. Of his four novels,

only *Sport of the Gods* (1902) deals mainly with Negro
characters—and here he implicity urges Negroes to submit to small town or plantation values—despite racial
injustices—since cities, by their very nature, are degen-
erate and corrupt. However kindly a view one may take of
Dunbar's problems in making his books acceptable to
white readers, one cannot escape the feeling that he was
himself one of his own worst oppressors.

With the relatively minor exceptions of Johnson,
Chesnutt, and Dunbar, Negro authors generally ignored
Negro folk life until it had begun passing out of existence.
But writers who gathered in Harlem in the 1920's—the
body of whose work is known as the Harlem Renaissance
—produced a flood of poems, short stories, novels, and
plays celebrating the low life of the cities. They were
encouraged in their efforts by a sizable white reading public which championed their cause. Unfortunately, much of
the literature of this period was second-rate stuff, pander-
ing to the sensation-seeking Jazz-Age readers who desired
to taste vicariously a life as different from their own as
they could find. With the onslaught of the Depression, the
vogue of the Negro died almost as swiftly as it had
emerged, suggesting perhaps that all the white public had
really wanted was a "fling," and now they had to get on
with the serious business of life—all of which points to
the somewhat tenuous grounds on which the Harlem
Renaissance was based.

To be sure, there was real need to record the life experience of the Negro masses—but the need was to record it
truthfully, not through the dark lenses of the "lush-life"
slummer trekking uptown to his favorite haunts. Unfortunately, in rebelling against the gentility, decorum, and
class snobbery of their predecessors, Renaissance writers
took an opposite tack that produced an equivalent distor-
tion. Taking their literary cues from the preoccupations of
the Jazz Age, they emphasized the Negro's "theatricality,"
his songs, his dances, and his social pleasures, nearly al-

ways to the exclusion of other important aspects of his life. The lower the socioeconomic position a fictional type occupied, the more likely he would be idealized. Pimps, prostitutes, porters, gamblers, vagabonds, migrant workers, and domestics were extolled as salt of the earth, while educated bourgeois Negroes were regarded with hostility and suspicion.

The same "primitive" animal qualities that previous generations of middle class writers had deplored or caricatured were now viewed as prime virtues while resplendent Africa and the "mysterious" characteristics of Negro blood converged to suggest a pristine superiority of spirit and character invulnerable to the contaminating decadence of Western civilization.

> What is Africa to me:
> Copper sun or scarlet sea,
> Jungle star or jungle track,
> Strong bronzed men, or regal black
> Women from whose loins I sprang
> When the birds of Eden sang?
> *One three centuries removed*
> *From the scenes his fathers loved,*
> *Spicy grove, cinnamon tree,*
> *What is Africa to me?*
>
> > *Countee Cullen*

The Harlem Renaissance was a swing to romanticism —sometimes dangerously racist, sometimes curiously exotic, but always self-congratulatory. The trouble is, of course, that romanticism by itself projects a cruelly distorted image of the Negro experience. No slum dweller, sharecropper, or washroom attendant experiences life more intensely for being exotic, poor, ignorant, or Negro. Whatever pleasure he derives from his social activities takes up only a minute proportion of his energies, so absorbed is he with the exigencies of physical survival. Harlem is not—and never was—a happy jungle, and to describe it as such only perpetuates the minstrel stereotype in another form.

Much of the impetus of the Renaissance came from forces outside Harlem. To the white American of the twenties, in an environment of burgeoning materialism and cultural mediocrity, the Negro represented something radiant and untouched and permanent in a world gone awry. His supposed singular pleasures and his freedom from Puritanical restraints suggested an appealing kind of release from the tensions of the recent war and the anxieties of readjustment. In the world of popular culture with its new craze for Negro dance steps, Negro jazz, and Negro entertainers, Harlem and similar communities became meccas for fun-seekers and tired whites who sought to resuscitate themselves in cabarets. Negroes responded in their time-honored way by donning the masks and assuming the postures expected of them.

Perhaps it was white writers who were most responsible for the way things happened. Popular accounts of Negro life began to appear everywhere: DuBose Heyward's *Mamba's Children* and *Porgy*, Sherwood Anderson's *Dark Laughter*, Carl Van Vechten's *Nigger Heaven*, to mention but a few. Eugene O'Neill's *The Dreamy Kid, All God's Chillun Got Wings*, and *The Emperor Jones* each had major characters who were Negroes.

Ironically, all of these literary goings-on came at a time when the Ku Klux Klan had attained the pinnacle of its success, extending itself beyond the boundaries of the South, when bloody race riots erupted in several major American cities, and when Negro lynchings, North and South, reached their most alarming numbers.

These events produced, in turn, an explosion of Negro nationalism. The most flamboyant symptom was Marcus Garvey's Universal Negro Improvement Association. Garvey, a West Indian who had come to the United States in 1916, urged the establishment of a Negro world nation in Africa with himself as provisional president. The UNIA encouraged the formation of co-operatively owned Negro businesses, banks, and apartment houses. Embodied in the movement as well was a hierarchical order of titled ranks (Dukes of the Niger, Duchesses of the Nile, etc.), and a projected army and nurse corps that Garvey called the Black Legion and the Black Cross. Garvey distributed decorations to his supporters freely (e.g., the Distinguished Order of Ethiopia and the Sublime Order of the Nile), and organized parades of his followers down city streets in lavish, splendid uniforms. He enjoyed immense popularity, especially among urban lower-class Negroes—a clear sign not only of the Negro's growing sense of alienation but of his demands for dignity and ethnic identity. Both Richard Wright and the playwright Theodore Ward have memorialized in their works the Garvey years of hope and despair.*

Other, more radical movements appealed to the Negro's dreams of freedom as well. In the late nineteen twenties and early thirties the American Communist Party called for an independent Negro state in the South. On the whole, communism made little headway with the majority of Negroes, who regarded it primarily as a white man's movement. If, however, one adds Du Bois's efforts to establish Pan African Congresses in Europe, one can sense the first real stirrings of black nationalism in the Negro community. This in turn was mirrored in the literature of the times. Why did it take more than fifty years after Emancipation for these attitudes to appear in Negro literature? What was it that prevented Negro authors from rendering more truthfully the lives of their people prior to the twenties? The answer appears to lie in the Negro's change from a simple peasant existence to that of a sophisticated city dweller. In the South from which he fled, the agrarian atmosphere and the more clearly defined caste barriers tended to isolate him. The traumatic memories of slavery and the devastation wrought by the Civil War engendered in the Negro a spirit of apathy and resigned despair. Richard Wright, in relating his youth in Mississippi, wrote the following:

* See Wright's novel *Lawd Today* (1963) and Ward's play *Big White Fog* (1940).

> After I had outlived the shocks of childhood, afte
> habit of reflection had been born in me, I used to
> over the strange absence of real kindness in Negroe,
> unstable was our tenderness, how timid our joy, how i
> our traditions, how hollow our memories, how lacking
> were in those intangible sentiments that bind man to m
> and how shallow was even our despair. . . . And when
> brooded upon the cultural barrenness of black life, I w
> dered if clean, positive tenderness, love, honor and loya
> and the capacity to remember were native to man.

Wright undoubtedly missed a great deal that was vari
and creative in Southern Negro life, and yet however
much Negroes may have dreamed the American dream,
its realization must have seemed hopelessly beyond their
reach.

The cities, on the other hand, with their bustle and
anarchy, afforded freedom of movement and closer contact with the political, social, and literary currents of the
time. Budding Negro authors found they had greater access to libraries and universities, and for the first time
they saw themselves wooed—and more than occasionally
patronized—by certain groups within the white community. It is true that odd assortments of radicals—Communists, Socialists, Marxists of one variety or another—had
their own political axes to grind, but the point is that they
introduced to Negroes a variety of emotional and intellectual experiences that they had seldom hitherto known in
their closed and insulated peasant lives. Most Negroes
rejected radical doctrines, but they recognized, in their
radical confrontations, the possibilities of whites and
blacks living together as equals. In describing his activities in the Chicago John Reed Club of the early thirties,
Richard Wright says that after his initial suspicions, he
found the experience as liberating as any he could remember. Likewise, white authors who sought out Negro
communities as happy hunting grounds for exotic materials provided Negro writers with opportunities for ob-

serving their methods and conversing with them on literary matters.

The nationalist aspects of the Renaissance literature of
the twenties—the fierce race pride, the constant sense of
ethnic identity, and the lure of Africa—remained a strong
factor in the writings of later Negro authors. Short-lived
it was, the Renaissance bore fruits in other ways as
well. The emphasis on the lives of the "little people" gave
way to the more somber naturalism of the thirties and
forties. The quaint and exotic urban settings of Harlem
gave way to more realistic accounts of city life. The
somewhat romanticized versions of Southern folk communities gave way to starker portrayals of Negro peasant
life. And the hand-me-down, devil-may-care attitudes of
Negro characters in Renaissance novels gave way to existential psychology in the works of the fifties and sixties.

Undoubtedly the most popular writer to emerge from
the Renaissance was the poet Langston Hughes, who was
born in Joplin, Missouri, in 1902. Although a good portion of his youth was spent in white communities in the
Midwest, Hughes was made aware of his heritage by his
grandmother, the widow of one of five Negroes who attacked Harper's Ferry with John Brown. He was also
related to John Mercer Langston, a Reconstruction Con-
gressman from Virginia and onetime dean of law at
Howard University.

It was in high school, in Cleveland, that Hughes first
began to write poetry. While on a train to Mexico to see
his father (who had fled the United States shortly after his
son's birth), Hughes wrote what is perhaps his finest
poem—one that he later dedicated to W. E. B. Du
Bois.

I've known rivers:
I've known rivers ancient as the world and older than the
flow of human blood in human veins.

My soul has grown deep like the rivers.

I bathed in the Euphrates when dawns were young.
I built my hut near the Congo and it lulled me to sleep.
I looked upon the Nile and raised pyramids above it.
I heard the singing of the Mississippi when Abe Lincoln
    went down to New Orleans, and I've seen its muddy
    bosom turn all golden in the sunset.

I've known rivers:
Ancient, dusky rivers.

My soul has grown deep like the rivers.

At the urging of his father, Hughes enrolled at Columbia University, but after a year of the academic life and a
variety of odd jobs, he signed as a merchant seaman and
sailed to West Africa and Europe. In 1924 and 1925 he
lived in Holland, France, and Italy, where again he supported himself with odd jobs. Upon returning to the
States, he worked as a busboy and doorman in Washington.

He was awarded the poetry prize in *Opportunity* in
1925. This won him the attention of Carl Van Vechten,
who used his good offices to get Hughes's first volume of
poetry, *The Weary Blues*, published the following year.
Another white patron, Vachel Lindsay, read some of
Hughes's poems at a public recital of his own verse.
Thereafter, Hughes found a growing white and Negro
audience, and in the next eight years he published four
volumes of poetry, a novel (*Not Without Laughter*,
1930), and a collection of short stories (*The Ways of
White Folks*, 1934). Meanwhile he enrolled at Lincoln
University and got his baccalaureate degree in 1929.

In the early 1930's Hughes joined the Communist
Party and headed a Party unit of Negro authors. This
earned him a trip to Russia in 1932 in which he was
expected to provide counsel for a Russian film (which
was never produced) on American Negro life. In 1935,

the first of his more than twenty plays, *Mulatto,* was produced on Broadway. In subsequent years his literary output and activities continued prodigious.

It is difficult to give a proper assessment of Hughes's
work because so much of its effect depends on an oral
interpretation and the physical presence of an audience.
Oddly, this is almost as true of his poems as of his plays,
despite the fact that from the beginning he experimented
with verse forms, diction, and typography. In a general
sort of way he is in the Whitman-Lindsay-Sandburg free-
verse tradition, yet despite this and his university education and wide cosmopolitan background, he is primarily a
folk artist who writes *for* the people he is writing *about.*
Even at his most ideological and didactic, he speaks with
directness, honesty, and understanding to those whose experiences he loves to share and record. There is something unmistakably genuine about his pride in the "little
people" whose lives, strivings, and endurance he celebrates, most often in their own voices, in jazz and gospel
rhythms and in visual patterns that dance before the eye
and demand to be read aloud.

> I'm gonna walk to de graveyard
> 'Hind ma friend, Miss Cora Lee.
> Gonna walk to de graveyard
> 'Hind ma dear friend Cora Lee.
> 'Cause when I'm dead some
> Body'll have to walk behind me.

Hughes's short stories and sketches have in them something of the great ghetto writer, Sholom Aleichem. His
characters, despite their defeats and humiliations, manage
usually to survive and discover a sometimes bitter, sometimes ironic humor in their situations and the absurd circumstances that encumber them. In point of fact,
Hughes's themes far transcend the deceptively simple nar-
ratives he writes; he writes really of the triumph of the
human spirit over adversity. And he is rarely condescending or sentimental.

His 1930 novel, *Not Without Laughter,* is a good ex-

ample. Hughes here gives an episodic account of a boy's
growing years in a small Kansas town. The dominant
character is the grandmother, who takes in white folks'
wash in order to help support her three daughters. The
eldest daughter, the wife of a bourgeois Negro adopts
middle-class postures, averring that this is the only way
Negroes can elevate themselves. The youngest, smarting
under the pro ncial prejudices of small-town life, leaves
home and becomes a prostitute—and later a great blues
singer. The middle daughter, the boy's mother, is married
to a "high yaller," a hedonistic, guitar-playing migratory
worker who returns to Kansas from time to time to stay
with the family. The novel details the changing relationships within the family, and the life of the Negro community—its churches, its social activities, its carnivals,
songs, jobs, and racial and class attitudes. Despite the
privations, the poverty, and the stinging racial prejudice,
the community possesses its own rich cultural resources—
a point of view Ralph Ellison would most strongly re-
assert in his essays of the fifties and sixties—and thus the
Negro is himself, in Hughes's view, not without laughter.

The author who won the most admiration from Negro
intellectuals in the twenties was probably the poet-novel-
ist, Jean Toomer. Toomer was born in 1894 in Washington, the son of a prominent New Orleans family (his
grandfather, F. S. Pinchback, was acting governor and
later senator from Louisiana during Reconstruction).
After attending Paul Laurence Dunbar High School in
Washington, Toomer studied law at the University of
Wisconsin, then attended the City College of New York.
He was apparently light-complexioned and handsome in a
conventional sort of way, and could easily have passed for
white, though for a long while he didn't. He had aspirations of becoming a composer, but he channeled his musical talents into his writings, which began to appear in a
succession of little experimental magazines around the
turn of the second decade.

The opposing strains of mysticism and realism in Toomer's writing had their counterparts in his professional and personal relationships. Although it seems that nearly all of his friends were white intellectuals, Toomer was among the first believers in négritude—glorifying the presumed special qualities of African blood. While still in his twenties, he sought to discover his roots in the rural South, and for a short time he taught school in Sparta, Georgia. In the early postwar years, he dabbled in psychoanalysis and yoga, and later joined the New York literary coterie of Kenneth Burke, Hart Crane, Gorham Munson, and Waldo Frank that championed the mystical teaching of Ouspensky's *Tertium Organum.* Some time around 1924, Toomer went to France, where he became a disciple of the Russian yoga mystic George Ivanovich Gurdjieff at his "Institute" at Fontainebleu. When he returned, Toomer attempted to spread his new-found vision in Harlem and Greenwich Village. Then he seems to have vanished.

Cane, his major work, was little noticed when it was first published in 1923, although a number of avant-garde writers like Munson, Frank, and Sherwood Anderson lauded it. Toomer's subsequent published output is negligible. There is a scattering of poems and prose pieces (mainly obscure), several essays, a fragment of a play, and a portion of a novel presumably in progress. He apparently wrote nothing after 1949 and is said finally to have denied he was a Negro; as Arna Bontemps has put it, he "faded into white obscurity." In his autobiography, Langston Hughes wrote that Toomer had been married twice, each time to a white woman, and that he had refused James Weldon Johnson permission to publish his works in a Negro anthology.

Cane is very nearly impossible to describe. At first glance, it seems a hodge podge of verse, songs, stories, and plays, yet there is a thematic unity celebrating the passions and instincts of black persons close to the soil as opposed to the corruption of their spirit and vitality in the cities. In idealizing the "primitivism" and négritude of the

Negro peasant, Toomer signaled the neoromantic attitudes of subsequent Negro authors in the twenties. Important too are Toomer's ambivalent attitudes about himself
and his South. No Negro writer has written of the South
with so much sense of pain and beauty inextricably
linked. For Toomer periodically injects memories and
images of the slave past into the very texture of his work,
and also attempts, often successfully, to arouse in his
reader unconscious longings for the mysterious lure of
Southern soil.

Is Toomer unconsciously saying that beauty resides in
the pain and suffering of black men? Is the mother earth
of Georgia to which he beckons his Negroes a death
dream that brings ultimate release? Are the busy social
and intellectual worlds of the city he portrays so enervat-
ing because they are so fulfilling, because they excite
areas of consciousness that had better be left alone? Are
passivity and withdrawal from modern life ultimate fulfillment? The paradox is inexplicable in rational terms,
but Toomer patterned his life in similar paradoxes. In
denying his Negroness in later years, Toomer may have
achieved the self-obliteration he seems to have urged in
Cane.

The son of lower-middle-class Jamaican parents,
Claude McKay came to the United States in 1912 after
publishing one volume of poems in the West Indies and
another in London. He attended a couple of American
colleges in the South and Midwest, and then gravitated to
radical political friendships in New York. In 1920, he
spent a year in England, where he published a third
volume of poems, *Spring in New Hampshire,* and then
returned to America to join Max Eastman as associate
editor of the Marxist periodical, *The Liberator.* McKay's
first American book of poems, *Harlem Shadows,* was published in 1922, although a number of the pieces included
had appeared in little magazines previously, some under
pseudonyms. Thereafter, McKay forsook poetry for prose,

publishing three novels, (*Home to Harlem*, 1928, *Banjo*, 1929; and *Banana Bottom*, 1933), a collection of short stories (*Gingertown*, 1932), an autobiography (*A Long Way From Home*, 1937), and a study of Harlem (*Harlem, Negro Metropolis*, 1940).

A considerable portion of McKay's life was spent in England, France, Germany, Russia, and several African countries, and he numbered among friends and acquaintances persons as diverse as Frank Harris, Art Young, Louis Untermeyer, Mary Heaton Vorse, Stuart Davis, George Bernard Shaw, H. G. Wells, Leon Trotsky, Genevieve Taggard, and some of the English Fabians.

McKay's best writings are found in his early Harlem poems, which alternate between a celebration of the Harlem proletariat and a clarion call for racial militancy. He wrote in conventional verse forms—especially the sonnet—and the contrast between his revolutionary ardor and the tight, traditional framework in which he encased it sometimes produced rather startling effects. Consider, for example, the poetic diction in the following sonnet, "The Lynching."

> His Spirit in smoke ascended to high heaven.
> His father, by the cruelest way of pain,
> Had bidden him to his bosom once again;
> The awful sin remained still unforgiven.
> All night a bright and solitary star
> (Perchance the one that ever guided him,
> Yet gave him up at last to Fate's wild whim)
> Hung pitifully o'er the swinging char.
> Day dawned, and soon the mixed crowds came to view
> The ghastly body swaying in the sun:
> The women thronged to look, but never a one
> Showed sorrow in her eyes of steely blue;
> And little lads, lynchers that were to be,
> Danced around the dreadful thing in fiendish glee.

McKay's novels, however, are not nearly so successful. Picaresque and episodic for the most part, they have an unfortunate propensity for reproducing minstrellike dialects in his major characters. *Home to Harlem*, for instance, describes the adventures, sexual and otherwise, of a caricatured army deserter during World War I. *Banjo*, in the same fashion, follows a group of Negro vagabonds around the cabarets and wharfs of Marseilles. *Banana Bottom*, his last novel, is better conceived and deals with a West Indian woman who deliberately elects to adopt the more primitive consciousness of the Negro community.

It is not improbable that British-educated West Indian Negroes, nurtured in a relatively race-free society, possess a greater sense of self-esteem than do their North American counterparts. McKay in any case achieved a high degree of success in the American Negro community. He suffered no feelings of inferiority, and evidently felt the barbs of American racism as fresh wounds. He leaped chauvinistically to the defense of his African ancestry as being something superior, while at the same time he apparently felt no qualms about associating with white intellectuals, with whom he probably felt more at ease. And yet at the root of McKay's radicalism is the ancient stereotype of the primitive Negro.

Another important Renaissance poet was Countee Cullen, who grew up in a Methodist parsonage in New York, attended New York University, and received an M.A. from Harvard in 1926. A strong academic orientation is apparent in most of his poems. Eschewing racial themes for the most part, Cullen worked a rigorous technical mastery over meter and rhyme and won plaudits and publication even while an undergraduate. Cullen modeled most of his verse on John Keats, whom he invoked on more than one occasion. But despite his efforts toward "universality," Cullen's most successful poetry is distinctly racial—something he himself subsequently came to realize.

Lord, I will live persuaded by mine own,
I cannot play recreant to these:
My spirit has come home, that sailed the doubtful seas.

It is generally accepted that Cullen's first volume of poems, *Color* (1925), is his best. Succeeding collections include *Copper Sun* (1927), *The Ballad of the Brown Girl* (1928), *The Black Christ* (1929), *The Medea and Other Poems* (1935), and *The Lost Zoo* (1940). In addition, he wrote several plays, and edited an anthology of Negro verse, *Caroling Dusk* (1927). Some of his lyrics have been set to music by Emerson Whithorne.

Cullen's only novel, *One Way to Heaven* (1932), deals with the adventures of a one-armed Negro gambler who "converts" periodically in Negro churches in order to support himself. It provides a first-rate picture of Negro urban churches—the best until James Baldwin's *Go Tell It On The Mountain* (1953). Interlaced in Cullen's narrative—not always successfully—is an account of a Negro socialite hostess who entertains white "liberals" and Negro literati and intelligentsia. Here Cullen anticipates Chester Himes's lampoon, *Pinktoes* (1965), by more than three decades.

Fenton Johnson, another Renaissance figure, started in an older school of dialect poets. His first collection, *A Little Dreaming* (1914), contains a rather pretentious three-hundred-line blank verse piece, "The Vision of Lazarus," and a number of other poems written in Dunbarlike dialect. When the war broke out, Johnson moved his tone and style closer to the Whitman-Masters-Sandburg free-verse school. James Weldon Johnson has placed him among the very first of a line of bitter, revolutionary social-protest poets.

> I am tired of work; I am tired of building up somebody
>   else's civilization.
> Let us take a rest, M'Lissy Jane.
> I will go down to the Last Chance Saloon, drink a gallon
>   or two of gin, shoot a game or two of dice and
>   sleep the rest of the night on one of Mike's barrels.
> You will let the old shanty go to rot, the white people's

clothes turn to dust, and the Calvary Baptist Church
   sink to the bottomless pit.
You will spend your days forgetting you married me and
   your nights hunting the warm gin Mike serves the
   ladies in the rear of the Last Chance Saloon.
Throw the children into the river; civilization has given
   us too many. It is better to die than to grow up
   and find that you are colored.
Pluck the stars out of the heavens. The stars mark our
   destiny. The stars marked my destiny.
I am tired of civilization.

Fenton Johnson's example extended well into the
1930's. Among those whom he may have influenced are
Langston Hughes, Richard Wright, Frank Marshall Davis
and Margaret Walker.

Several Renaissance novelists deserve mention as well.
Among these are the satirists George Schuyler and Wal-
lace Thurman. Schuyler's novel, *Black No More* (1931),
relates the devastating effects on the national culture
when an electrical treatment is discovered that can transform Negroes into paler versions of Caucasians. Thurman's novel, *Infants of the Spring* (1932), is an attack on
professional Negro intellectuals, literati, and Bohemians
who assemble periodically at Niggeratti Manor to con-
verse and exchange opinions. Neither novel is particularly
distinguished, but they do represent attempts by Negro
authors to employ the medium of satire as a means of protest.

One of the best craftsmen of the Renaissance was Nella
Larsen. Her novels deal with the affairs of the Negro
middle class, which appear to center on the problem of
"passing." Perhaps the kindest that can be said of them is
that they treat this ancient theme with considerably
greater sophistication than preceding generations. *Quicksand* (1928), for example, relates the story of a highly
intelligent woman of mixed parentage whose intense but
repressed sexuality brings about her downfall. The nar-

rative moves from Chicago to New York, to Copenhagen, back again to Chicago, and finally to the rural deep South, where the heroine is engulfed in the day-to-day torpor of a fundamentalist peasant community. The novel smacks in places of Edith Wharton's *House of Mirth*, soap opera, and *Abie's Irish Rose*—as Helga Crane is constantly faced with decisions about whom she should marry, and of which racial stock. Somehow one cannot imagine a writer today regarding his heroine's physical desires as the quicksand of her life. Yet if one grants such an assumption, the novel unfolds skillfully. The main character is beautifully understood, and the prose flows easily. Unfortunately for Nella Larsen, her novel appeared in a decade that stressed primitivism and the urgency of the senses. Nor have readers of a subsequent generation regarded sympathetically the problems of the Negro middle class.

With the advent of the Depression, the number and quality of Negro writers declined. The idea of the Negro as some kind of pristine exotic had seen its day, and the few noteworthy Negro writers assumed more class-conscious attitudes. Race pride was to a certain extent played down, and Negro oppression was viewed as part of a larger picture of capitalist exploitation of the masses.

> Listen, you drawing men
> I want a picture of a starving black
> I want a picture of a starving white
> Show them bitterly fighting down on the dark soil
> Let their faces be lit by hate
> Above there will stand
> The rich plantation owner, holder of the land
> A whip in his red fist
> Show his pockets bulging with dollars spilled
> From the ragged trousers of the fighting men
> And I shall call it
> "Portrait of the Cotton South."
>
> *Frank Marshall Davis*

The postwar years have seen a new flowering and diversity of Negro letters, against the background of

libertarian court decisions, civil rights legislation, the rise
of new African states, Negro nationalism, and ghetto uprisings in some of the major American cities. And it is
with this period that the principal portions of this book
will be concerned. But it would be well to remember that
the new Negro Renaissance—if that is what it may be
called—was not created out of a vacuum. The Harlem
Renaissance, by focusing attention on the Negro masses,
opened up areas of subject matter that had scarcely ever
before been treated. And in rejecting the traditional
values of the white middle class, these writers also rejected traditional modes of expression that had hitherto
made so much Negro writing appear sterile and uncon-
vincing, and opened the way to experimentation in a variety of literary forms.

Chapter III
Migration: William Attaway and Blood on the Forge

There persists to this day a widely held belief that the deep South, with its brutal caste system and its savage history of racial atrocities, represents for Negroes an image of steaming hell. Such a view is constantly reinforced by spokesmen for civil rights organizations and activists of various liberal persuasions. It serves their political convenience and humanitarian goals, which is all to the good, but unfortunately it muddles their thinking. For it is grounded on the assumption that people are political and economic entities whose motivations and behavior may be simplistically understood. Since Negroes have been systematically exploited and oppressed in the South, it follows they must hate

47

the South that has persecuted them. There are partial truths here—how else explain the vast northward migrations that have been taking place over the past fifty or so years? But what of the large numbers who have stayed behind? Partial truths are not satisfactory to the artist, for he understands that people often leave the place of their origins not simply out of hatred, but because they want to continue to love their homes. And they carry their love with them to the dismal ghettos of the North and cherish it all the more for their adversity. Jean Toomer, for all his woozy romanticism, persuades because his South represents a heartfelt need, and even racial militants like Richard Wright, may, on occasion, speak lyrically of "down-home" times. They miss especially the soil, the seasons, the sense of community they once knew; they regale one another with stories and fables and legends of family, friends, and relatives they left behind; and they attempt to adapt their older ways to the anarchy of city life. Frequently they return South for visits in order to renew themselves.

Calvin Hernton, in a recent book of essays, describes the mixed feelings of some of these visitors:

> The fact that Negroes are alienated from the broader life of the South and its deeper mysteries does not frequently pull them away, but binds them ever more closely to the bosom of Down-Home. The South is the mother-matrix out of which and in which the Negro's mind has been fashioned; it is at the same time the festering ache in the republic of his heart. This, more than anything else, is why they go back.

Such ambivalence has seldom been expressed with more skill or emotional impact than in William Attaway's *Blood on the Forge* (1941), a narrative describing the first stage of the Negro's journey North from his ancestral home. It recounts the experiences of the three brothers Moss in a steel-mill town in western Pennsylvania after leaving their Kentucky hill-country tenant farm during World War I. In the course of the novel one of the broth-

ers is killed, and as the book closes the two remaining
brothers move on to the city, where they hope to acquire
new roots.

The novel not only records a critical moment in the
Negro's history but expands its significance by reference
to some of the larger events of the American experience.
It takes into account the looming strife between incipient
labor unions and the steel companies, the psychology and
culture of east European immigrants as they work alongside Southern Negroes, and the specific work conditions
under which they all struggle. But it would be a mistake
to regard *Blood on the Forge* as a tract, for Attaway
rendered the usual subject matter of the proletarian novel
into a work of art. He transcended his materials to describe a strange odyssey of the human spirit—without
losing several familiar sociological truths. Indeed, what
may puzzle the reader is a certain cold realism combined
with what can only be described as fervored romantic
pessimism.

The failure of the novel to attain popularity may perhaps be ascribed to this paradoxical achievement. On the
face of it, *Blood on the Forge*—even its title—suggests
simply another of the interminable working-class novels
dealing with the downtrodden and their efforts to succeed
to a dignified life. Or perhaps the novel was read as naturalistic fiction, but because it did not quite fit the "uplift" formula of its day, it was ignored and relegated to the
dustbin of the ideologically confused. Whatever the reasons, it is clear that neither the "aesthetes" who wanted
their art to eschew all sociological comment, nor the "socially committed' who wanted their art to point the way,
would have looked favorably on *Blood on the Forge*,
since in form and subject matter it seems to lie somewhere in a no man's land. Attaway has ideological axes to
grind, but they are honed in peculiarly traditional American accents. He urges the primacy of the life of the soil
over the life-denying machine, and projects the American
image of men of different nationalities and colors working

and living together. For all that, his books may have appeared a little foreign to American readers. Possibly the publication of Richard Wright's more sensational *Native Son* the preceding year had something to do with it. Wright's novel was less polished, but it contained rather startling revelations for white readers unused to racial complexities. The American reading public apparently could take only one Negro at a time. Wright became a "spokesman"; Attaway never published another novel.

Attaway prepared the way for *Blood on the Forge* with *Let Me Breathe Thunder*, a novel he published two years earlier in 1939. In one sense Attaway is less inhibited in his first book because he is writing primarily about white characters whose point of view would not be readily understood as racial. Yet his protagonists, hobo migrant farm workers, are Negroes under the skin—pariahs, consumed at the same time with wanderlust and the desire to stay put. Their agony is a Negro agony, and their allusions to race problems are more "inside" than Attaway might have cared to admit. They speak on more than one occasion of interracial sex and its conspiratorial acceptance in middle-class communities, of the various kinds of racial prejudice they meet throughout the country— and the fact that only hoboes do not appear to discriminate; of the private humiliations "outsiders" experience in a bourgeois milieu, and above all of their uneasiness in accommodating themselves to the patterns of American life, and their desire not to do so. They are the alienated, the uncommitted, whose discontents may one day be marshaled toward revolution—but not necessarily of the doctrinaire, ideological variety. They do not yet know what they want, but they know what they dislike. Once they are aware of what they seek, they are perhaps capable of changing their world.

Attaway here does not understand his people. His solution, like Toomer's, is a return to the soil. A character named Sampson, who owns orchards and farm lands, has suffered considerably during his life; his wife and sons have died and he lives alone with an adolescent daughter. But his strong sense of identification with the land serves to renew him and give him perspective and emotional balance. Sampson is portrayed most sympathetically, but Attaway cannot make him ring altogether true. And the hoboes whom he asks to stay with him on the land cannot believe in him either; as the novel closes, they leave to try their luck elsewhere. Attaway's inability to make Sampson believable stems as much from anachronism as from failure of craftmanship. The American dream of the independent farmer was outmoded by the Depression years, and Attaway was simply unable to cope with his nostalgia.

The plot of *Let Me Breathe Thunder* is unsophisticated and sometimes Hollywoodishly sentimental. It deals with two hardened migratory farm workers in Washington State who adopt as their companion a lost, orphaned ten-year-old Mexican-American youth. Hi Boy, the name they have given him, speaks no English at first, rides the rods with them, and comes to adore Step, the more romantic and volatile of the two. At one point Hi Boy grinds a fork into his hand in order to prove to Step (who rather disapproves of the child as an unnecessary encumbrage) that he has the fortitude to bear the vicissitudes of the migratory life. The three companions settle later on Sampson's farm in Yakima, where Step rather reluctantly falls in love with Anna, Sampson's daughter. Their place of assignation is the home of a Negro woman, Mag, who owns brothels and considerable property in Yakima. In the course of events, Anna is rather dramatically discovered awaiting Step in Mag's house, and Step and his companion and Hi Boy flee in a boxcar. As they travel east across the country, Hi Boy's hand swells up from his self-inflicted wound. The men do everything they can to save him but he dies. Step and his companion conceal the body under a tarpaulin in a boxcar headed for New Mexico, Hi Boy's birthplace, then continue east to Kansas to seek new work.

The novel celebrates the loyalty and decency of men on the move, and the essential virtues of the life of the soil. Attaway's Negro themes, as we have seen, are muted and disguised, which allows him to speak the language of protest without using its rhetoric. In shying away from making his main characters Negroes, Attaway was perhaps fearful of having his novel labeled protest fiction. The two Negro characters who do appear in the novel have no especial "Negro" traits, and although one of them is nearly lynched for the supposed attempted rape of a white girl, scarcely any allusion is made to his race. It appears as if Attaway were bending over backwards to assure his readers that he is not writing "sociology." Such a position is absurd, since any reader would naturally associate lynchings and imaginary sex crimes with race. The novel falters on other counts: the characters rarely spring to life, and their situations vaguely suggest those Steinbeck described two years earlier in *Of Mice and Men*. Yet for all that, the narrative does possess a certain verve, and the prose is economical and clean in the Hemingway manner —objective but replete with undertones of irony and sadness.

In *Blood on the Forge*, the Hemingway style is transformed by Negro tones and rhythms. As the novel traces the deterioration of the Negro peasant under the crush of industrial life, Attaway rings changing images of the natural Southern landscape against the hearths, blast furnaces, and smoking chimneys of the steel-mill town. Implicit in the language is a kind of hell-death-decay imagery. His "green men" glance about them upon their arrival in Allegheny County and remember their former homes, the red clay hills, where "there was growing things everywhere and crab-apple trees bunched—stunted but beautiful." What they see now is an "ugly, smoking hell out of a backwoods preacher's sermon." Later they ask, "Where are the trees? They so far away on the tops of the low mountains that they look like the fringe on a black wear-me-to-a-wake dress held upside down against the sky."

Attaway foreshadows the disintegration of black men under these conditions when the brothers, on their first day in the Pennsylvania community, spy a Negro whore approaching them on the street. At first they are attracted, but as she passes alongside, they are nearly overcome by a sickening odor. They are told afterward that one of her breasts is rotting away.

The reduction of the brothers begins almost immediately. Surrounded by rusty iron towers, brick stacks, magnets, traveling cranes, and steam shovels, they appear even to themselves physically diminished in size:

> They had always thought of [Mat, the eldest] as big and powerful as a swamp tree. Now, in their eyes, he was getting smaller and smaller. Like spiral worms, all their egos had curled under pressure from the giants around them. Sooner or later it came to all the green men.

Attaway does not, however, confine this effect entirely to Negroes. The other workers in the mills—Irish, Italians, Slovaks, and Ukrainians—in one sense make better adjustments to industrial life. They raise families—for them their children are "growing things"—while the Negroes make no attempt to send home for their wives and children. Yet the white workers fare scarcely better: their children fornicate and commit incest in the weeds outside their homes, and their grown daughters become whores.

Steel, the indestructible symbol of industry, assumes a powerful impersonal force, brutalizing and degrading to the human spirit.

> The fire and flow of metal seemed an eternal act which had grown beyond men's control. It was not to be compared with crops that one man nursed to growth and ate at his own table. The nearness of a farmer to his farm was easily understood. But no man was close to steel. It was shipped across endless tracks to all the world. On the consignment slips were Chicago, Los Angeles, New York, rails for South America, tin for Africa, tool steel for Europe. This hard metal held up the new world. Some were shortsighted and thought they understood. Steel is born in

the flames and sent out to live and grow old. It comes back
to the flames and has a new birth. But no one man could
calculate its beginning or end. It was old as the earth. It
would end when the earth ended. It seemed deathless.

But if Attaway deplores the evils of the industrial North,
he does not conversely romanticize the virtues of the pastoral South. Unlike Toomer, he savagely portrays the
South as being too oppressive for Negroes. In the first
part of the novel the three brothers live together (with
Hattie, Mat's wife) as tenant farmers in the Kentucky red-
clay hills. They are on the verge of starvation and en-
slaved in debt. Even farming is largely useless because
most of the topsoil has been washed away over the course
of years. What remains for the brothers is the memory,
the idea, the "dream" of the land as it must have been
before they and the land were exploited by racist owners.
The erosion of the land suggests the erosion of their
morale which, in a sense, washes them off the land. The
immediate cause of their hasty departure, however, is a
beating administered by Mat to a white overseer. In order
to escape the inevitable lynch mob, the brothers go North
to the steel mills. Circumstances keep Mat from taking
Hattie along, and Mat's separation from his wife signals
the beginning of the dissolution of their family life.

The Kentucky sequence serves to introduce the major
characters, who together suggest a composite Negro folk
personality. Melody, who will manage best in the ordeal
ahead, is sensitive and poetic. He is so named because of
his skill with the guitar and because he is capable of
articulating in song the folk life of the peasant. Chinatown
is simple, lazy, sensual, and hedonistic. He lives by outward symbols; his greatest source of pride is his gold
tooth, because, as he puts it later, it shines and smiles at
him. Mat, the dominant figure of the group, is huge,
brooding, and sullen. All his life he has suffered insults
and humiliation at the hands of whites, but he has managed for the most part to suppress his rage and adopt a
glazed expression when he is most hurt. An intensely reli-

gious man, Mat reads the Bible constantly to discover the causes of his agony. He believes he is cursed because he was conceived in sin, and that the curse has manifested itself in Hattie's inability to give birth to a child. Six times pregnant, Hattie has "dropped" her baby each time before it was born—and this is the central metaphor that supports Attaway's main theme, for Hattie's infertility corresponds to the infertility of the Southern soil that can no longer give sustenance to Negro life. Hence the brothers seek to sink roots in soil elsewhere. Insofar as they cannot do so, they will diminish and wither.

The second part of the novel relates the journey of the brothers to Pennsylvania—crouched and huddled in a dark boxcar with numerous other Negroes who are being brought North to work in mills.

> Squatted on the straw-spread floor of a boxcar, bunched up like hogs headed for market, riding in the dark for what might have been years, knowing time only as dippers of warm water gulped whenever they were awake, helpless and dropping because they were headed into the unknown and there was no sun, they forgot even that they had eyes in their heads and crawled around in the boxcar, as though it were a solid thing of blackness.

The screech, the rattle, the roar of the train, the fetid air, the smell of urine demoralized the men. "The misery that stemmed from them was a mass experience." Not even Mat could "defend his identity against the pack." Chinatown whimpers, terrified that someone in the dark may try to steal his gold tooth. He tells Melody that "without it I ain't nobody." Nor can Melody play his guitar and sing in the deafening noise. It is as if the train journey has suddenly and shockingly severed them from all connection with the past—a feeling not unlike what their African ancestors must have experienced in the holds of the slave ships. Yet in another sense the boxcar is a kind of womb preparing to disgorge them into a new life.

But the life of the steel mills is even more dehumanizing than the one they have fled. Once the green men overcome their initial bewilderment at the sterile, ugly grayness of the community, they attempt to acclimate themselves. They learn from bunkhouse talk how to survive in their dangerous work. They feel the hostility of the white workers, who fear—with justification—that the Negroes have been transported North in order to weaken the union. They learn above all the drudgery of the mill, the tedium, the immense physical stamina required of steel workers on twelve-hour shifts. Their off hours at first are spent sleeping, but soon they begin to enjoy dice games in the bunkhouses, drinking corn whiskey, "whoring" in Mex Town, and attending dog fights. Even Mat allows himself to be drawn into these frivolities after he learns by letter that Hattie has lost her seventh baby. Melody has meanwhile fallen in love with a fifteen-year-old Mexican-American prostitute, Anna, whose earthy nature is adulterated somewhat by her pathetic longings for dance-hall dresses and high-heeled shoes. When Melody fails to satisfy her at their first encounter, she throws herself at Mat, whose brute strength and courage in a melee at the dog fights had rescued her from physical harm.

In certain respects Mat appears to adjust more easily to the life of a steel worker than his brothers. His physical strength is put to the test, and he proves himself more than equal to it. He wins a grudging respect among his fellow workers, and his self-abasement under the glare of the white man seems to disappear. Yet after breaking with his puritanical, Bible-oriented moorings, Mat will need something more than the knowledge that he can stand up to any white man in order to sustain his emotional balance.

Chinatown, on the other hand, makes the worst adjustment. His gold tooth does not count for much in the gray steel community. Nor can he, in his casual Southern way, easily withstand the pressures and tensions of the world he has entered. He misses the out-of-doors, the feel of the earth beneath his bare feet, the sun and the warmth. Melody tries to keep the brothers together but is troubled by a sense of loss. He cannot play his guitar and sing as he once did. He is aware of a need for other melodies, other rhythms in his new environment, yet he cannot quite catch them. His impotence with Anna suggests the signal impotence of all three brothers in their new life.

There is a remarkable soliloquy in this section of the novel, delivered by a crippled Negro named Smothers. Smothers has lost the use of his legs in an accident in the mills some years before, but he is retained on the job by the steel company as a watchman. He is regarded tolerantly by his fellow workers despite his obsessive tirades against steel. Smothers is prophetic—a crippled Tiresias announcing the apocalypse if men persist in their materialist pursuits. His harangues restate the view implicit at the start of the novel that the earth gives moral and spiritual sustenance to men, and that its destruction transgresses nature and denies men their potentialities. On one occasion he rises in the bunkhouse to utter the following words:

It's wrong to tear up the ground and melt it up in the furnace. Ground don't like it. It's the hell-and-devil kind of work. Guy ain't satisfied with usin' the stuff that was put here for him to use—stuff on top of the earth. Now he got to git busy and melt up the ground itself. Ground don't like it, I tells you. Now they'll be folks laugh when I say the ground got feelin'. But I knows what it is I'm talkin' about. All the time I listen real hard and git scared when the iron blast holler to git loose, an' them big redhead blooms screamin' like the very heart o' the earth caught between them rollers. It jest ain't right. . . .

Can't blame the ground none. It give warnin'. Yessir, they was warnin' give a long time ago. Folks say one night there's somethin' fall right outen the sky, blazin' down, lightin' up this ol' river in the black o' night. . . . A solid hunk o' iron it be, big around as a house, fused together like it been worked by a puddler with a arm size of a hundred-foot crane. Where it come from? Where this fur-

nace in the sky? You don't know. I don't know. But it
were a warning to quit meltin' up the ground.

Later in the same section, Attaway describes a dog
fight which the brothers attend along with other workers.
The event is particularly savage but evidently serves to
relieve the spectators of their built-up murderous frustrations. Its effect on Mat, however, is quite the opposite, as
he begins to strike out wildly and indiscriminately at the
other workers like a starved dog loosed from its leash.

The passage of time brings the further decline of the
brothers. Mat has rented a shack and is now living with
Anna. He has given up all thoughts of sending for Hattie
and has left his Bible behind in the bunkhouse. Melody
broods over the loss of Anna and schemes to get her
back. He calls on her while Mat is working at the mill.
Anna suspects his motives, and her suspicions are confirmed when he announces that he wants to give Mat a
letter from Hattie. Anna wrestles with him to take the
letter away from him. Exhausted and unsuccessful, she
gives up the fight and she and Melody make love. It soon
becomes clear that Anna is not happy living with Mat,
who does not allow her to go out and show off the
sequined dress and high-heeled shoes he bought her with
money he had been saving for Hattie. The next day Anna
disappears, and when she returns two days later Mat assumes she has been "lying" with someone and beats her
savagely. Actually she has been lying on the hills near the
big homes of wealthy townspeople, fantasying that she is
the mistress of a rich man.

Events move swiftly now. Melody has an accident at
the mill which severely damages his guitar-playing hand.
Then Mat is arrested in Pittsburgh for attempting to kill a
man. Melody drives to Pittsburgh to bail him out, and on
the return trip Mat, crushed and defeated, tells him that
Anna no longer truly gives herself to him.

The portents of disaster build. Again steel serves as the
underlying metaphor to suggest the hellish antilife man
has created, and it is again the raving Smothers who calls

up the image of a monster that demands human sacrifice. Smothers senses impending death. "Ever'body better be on the lookout. Steel liable to git somebody today. I got a deep feelin' in my bones," he says. The men laugh and Bo, the foreman, promises Smothers, "If it's you . . . we make you up into watch fobs. The boys round the bunkhouse'll wear you across their vests for luck." Smothers tells the hair-raising story of how he lost his legs in the mill and how afterward, "All the time in the hospital I kin hear that steel talkin' . . . I kin hear that steel laughin' an' talkin' till it fit to bust my head clean open . . . I kin hear when cold steel whisper all the time and hot roll steel scream like hell. *It's a sin to melt up the ground. . . .*"

Melody, too, has come to sense steel as a death god. "Suddenly Melody was aware of the warning. He started up. There was great danger. Something screamed it inside him. . . . Perhaps the monster had gotten tired of an occasional victim. Perhaps he was about to break his chains. He would destroy masses of men, flesh, bones and blood, leaving only names to bury."

And then there is a blinding flash, followed by "a mushroom cloud, streaked with whirling red fire. . . ." Several workers, Smothers included, are killed. Chinatown is blinded.

In a sense each of the brothers has now been rendered impotent: Chinatown, who lives by outward symbols, can no longer see; Melody, who lives through his music, can no longer play the guitar; and Mat has become a hulking shell of a man because Anna no longer loves him. All three brothers go to live with Anna. She no longer sleeps with Mat, but takes care of Chinatown, whose eyes are like "old eggs rotting in their ragged half shells, purple and revolting."

Racial tensions are rising in the town. The union is moving toward a strike and the steel interests are countering by bringing more Negroes in from the South. Negro leaders have been bought off and are directing Negro workers not to join the union. Meanwhile the depleted Mat has taken to walking alone among the hills on the edge of town. On one occasion he is approached by the law and sworn in as a deputy, ostensibly to maintain order but really to help break the forthcoming strike. He views this as an opportunity to redeem his faltering manhood with Anna—and at the same time, unconsciously, to wreak his vengeance on whites.

On the day of the strike, Melody, in order to bolster Chinatown's dashed ego, takes him to a brothel. Inadvertently he discovers Anna has been secretly working there nights, and rushes back to the shack to accuse her—and to beg her to run away with him. Suddenly Mat returns. Overhearing their conversation, he savagely beats Anna into a heap, then shambles back to town and brutally provokes some of the strikers on orders of the sheriff. In the ensuing melee, Mat kills and injures a number of them before he is himself hacked down.

The novel closes on Melody and Chinatown headed for Pittsburgh, where they will begin life anew.

Part of the strength of this final section of the novel lies in Attaway's generally successful fusion of naturalistic and metaphysical elements. The social and economic forces that drive the brothers from the Kentucky hills and divide the steel community in bloody conflict are in themselves crimes against nature. The same pride and greed that destroy the soil manifest themselves again as racial tension and industrial strife. Attaway focuses these perceptions on Mat just prior to his death. Having been rejected by Anna, Mat tries to redeem his ego by identifying himself with steel.

> Big Mat looked at the mills, and the big feelings were lifting him high in the air. He was big as God Almighty. . . . He could have spit and quenched a blast furnace. . . . Smothers had been a liar. Steel couldn't curse a man. Steel couldn't hurt him. He was the riding boss. How could those dead mills touch him? With his strength he could relight their fires or he could let them lie cold.

But like some epic Greek hero, Mat recognizes his *hubris* at the moment of his death, and intuits that his brutality in attacking the workers is just like the brutality to which he himself had been subjected in the South. And he recognizes too that the young Slav who is striking at him with a pickaxe handle is not unlike the Mat who struck out violently at a white man in Kentucky. Like Oedipus, Mat is his own persecutor and victim.

Unfortunately, for Mat (and the Negro by implication) vision comes too late. Attaway contrasts Mat's vision at death to Chinatown's continuing blindness in life. On the train that carries Melody and Chinatown to Pittsburgh, the brothers meet a blind Negro soldier who used to be a steel worker. When Chinatown asks why he left the mills, the soldier explains that he responded to a deep feeling inside him—a sound of guns. He tells Chinatown that he too can hear the guns if he listens carefully. Chinatown strains, and "their noise came over the rumble of the train."

> "Sound like somethin' big an' important that a fella's missin', don't it?" asked the soldier.
> Chinatown nodded.
> Melody watched the nod. He looked at the two blind men closely. Their heads cocked to one side, listening for sounds that didn't exist. They were twins.

And so the blind lead the blind. Just as the soldier was lured away from home by the nonexistent glory of war, so Melody and his brothers have been seduced from their homes by promises of freedom and security in the North. And thus it would always be for men like Chinatown and the soldier.

One of the most significant passages in the novel describes a strange ritual some of the workers perform after Smothers' death. It will be recalled that prior to the explosion in the mill, Bo says that if Smothers were to die, the men would use his remains for watch fobs. The men carry out their promise one day in the bunkhouse.

[Bo] sat on the floor in the middle of an intent audience. No one spoke. Their attention was for Bo and for what he did. Between his legs was a pile of little steel scraps. In front of him burned a tin of canned heat. Bo put a steel dish on the heat. Into the dish went a few pieces of lead. Then he sat back to wait.

.   .   .   .

For twenty minutes they sat. Nothing sounded but the sudden scrape of a boot against the grain of the floor. Then the massed breathing of the men began to grow until it whistled. A watch in someone's pocket ticked louder and louder. The creak of the bunkhouse in the changing air came now and again. Each man heard his own heart circling its own blood. So what was silence spoke louder and louder.

Then the time was up. The lead cupped the bottom of the dish, a heavy dust scumming its brightness. With ceremony Bo broke that scum. Then out of his pocket came the little chains. A drop of lead fastened each chain to one of the steel scraps. Shortly he was through. Bo began to pass out these newly crested watch fobs. Afterward the group broke up.

Attaway ends his novel on a note of defeat. Yet even in defeat, his protagonists persist—though not very hopefully—in their struggle for survival and identity. The brothers' renewed search for the good life seems doomed from the start. One knows that the entire cycle of hope, passion, and defeat will begin again with such persons as the blind "twins," Chinatown and the soldier—blind because they will continue to be deluded by unattainable dreams and promises.

One wonders, naturally, whether their author was himself as overcome with the hopelessness of his prognosis. Born in Mississippi in 1912, the son of a physician, Attaway was himself part of the great migration North. He attended public schools in Chicago and, after an interim as a hobo, he worked at a variety of jobs before returning to the University of Illinois to complete his education. It was in high school, Attaway writes, that he

developed an interest in becoming an author. He had always assumed that Negro success was to be won in genteel professions like medicine, but upon first reading
Langston Hughes, his outlook was transformed. Prior to
the appearance of his two novels, he published little. His
first novel, as we have seen, was promising; his second, a
classic of its kind. Why then did Attaway stop writing
fiction? He was only twenty-nine when *Blood on the
Forge* appeared. It is, of course, always hazardous to
guess at the motives of a writer, but possibly some clues
may be found in the works themselves.

It is first of all clear that Attaway had no intention of
writing "race" fiction. He did not want his novels to stop
short at "protest," but rather hoped to make some grand
metaphysical statement about the conditions of life and
human experience, in which, possibly, Negro characters
figured. But such a wholly laudable ambition was not, as
has already been suggested, something the American reading public was prepared to accept from a Negro author—
especially at the outset of World War II, when the great
tasks ahead appeared to lie more in action and less in
reflection. Attaway may simply have been discouraged at
the response to his book—and quit.

Another alternative, however, suggests itself. It is perhaps in the realm of ideas that we may look for the source
of Attaway's arrested artistic development. Basically
Attaway is a romantic. *Let Me Breathe Thunder,* for all
its praise of stable family life and the virtues of farming,
ultimately celebrates the free-wheeling bohemianism of
hoboes—and Attaway, by manipulating his plot this way
and that, manages to free his protagonists from any social
and moral obligations. In another romantic vein, *Blood on
the Forge* projects the myth of the "good" soil corrupted
by man's greed, whose logical absurdity manifests itself in
the manufacture of steel. While no one would deny that
the excesses of American capitalism have produced cruel
and dehumanizing injustices, it is hard, after Darwin, to
ascribe moral virtues to nature. And since it is scarcely

possible any longer to look to nature as something apart and holy, Attaway may well have written himself out of subject matter.

And yet if one grants Attaway his premises, it is undeniable that he has written a beautiful and moving novel. Nor can one deny that his vision of earth as sanctified remains persistently embedded in the American *mythos*. It is, after all, out of such nostalgia that art is created.

Since the appearance of his books, Attaway has been associated with the radio and television industry. His last published works have been the liner notes on Harry Belafonte record jackets.

Chapter IV

Richard Wright: <u>Native Son</u> and Three Kinds of Revolution

Richard Wright's *Native Son* (1940) represents a watershed in Negro letters. It seized the imagination of readers and catapulted its author into fame, making him a source of controversy for years to come—a controversy that has not yet subsided. The initial reaction was shock. Wright's account of a shiftless, seemingly apathetic slum boy who harbored an obsessive hatred of whites came as a startling revelation even to the most liberal of white readers—who, when they thought of Negroes at all, tended to regard them benignly as persons just like themselves in black skins. Perhaps even more shocking was Wright's apparent view that the brutal murders Bigger commits in celebration of his hatred are, after all, the logical outcome of his absurd position in American life. Wright was not, of course, condoning violence, but he *was* saying that the alternative behavior, for the majority of slum Negroes, was dumb submission to a dehumanizing lot. Moreover, Wright further startled white (and Negro) readers by taking as his central figure the stereotyped "nigger" (the name Bigger is suggestive), whose crimes against a white girl were vaguely sexual in origin. That any Negro author should want to aggravate the paranoid fantasies of racist extremists seemed to some readers almost beyond belief.

Needless to say, white and Negro critics rushed to print, praising or condemning the novel, and still do. And it is not surprising that some of Wright's harshest critics were Negroes. He did not give a true picture of the Negro, they said, but rather a monstrous version of the stereotype that has condemned the vast majority of law-abiding members of their race to live in subhuman conditions (this was precisely Wright's point—that subhuman conditions produce subhuman persons). They protested additionally that Wright's determinism or communism (he was a Party member at the time) distorted reality, since whites and Negroes have often in history transcended their debased environments. Was not Wright himself born into grinding poverty? Here the critics may have had a point, but Wright was writing not about those "transcended" Negroes, but rather about the many more who had remained mired in the despair and hopelessness of the ghettos.

Whatever the case, on rereading the novel some twenty-five years later, one finds that much of the criticism seems clearly beside the point. What Wright was describing, although he may not have known it at the time, was his vision of modern man.

In his entire writing career, Wright produced twelve books (two were published posthumously), and it is astonishing how each, despite Wright's shifting political and philosophical positions, picks up on one or another of the

main strands of *Native Son.* In order to understand this
better, it is first essential to ask something about the man,
for Wright embodied in his own life much that is apparently contradictory in his works. Indeed, in a manner of
speaking, Wright's history echoes the Negro's history in
microcosm, in that it spans the years of Southern feudal-
ism, the Northern urban migration, and the international
arena of black African politics. If there is a theme to
Wright's life, it is freedom, and the various means he took
to achieve it were conditioned by his circumstances.

He was born the son of a tenant farmer outside
Natchez in September, 1908. When he was six, his father
abandoned his family and his mother was left in sole
charge of Richard and his younger brother. For the next
ten or so years Ella Wright and her two children trekked
across Mississippi, Tennessee, and back again to Mississippi in search of a permanent home. For a brief period
Richard was placed in an orphanage, and just prior to his
final departure from Mississippi at the age of fifteen, he
lived for several years with his mother's parents at their
home in Jackson. His entire formal education consisted of
nine years of public schooling, and up until the age of
twelve he had not spent one year in the same school.

It is impossible to overestimate the importance of these
Southern years, for not only did they provide Wright with
the subject matter of many of his works, but they suggested to him all his major themes, regardless of whether
he was writing about the urban proletariat in Chicago or
the nationalist upheavals on the west coast of Africa.

He was, like all Americans, a creature of the American
dream of justice and equality for all men, and each of his
works is informed by this idea. His adoption of communism years later was only a variation on this theme.
Wright did not believe that freedom could be attained
under the present political conditions of American life.

But being a Negro, he was not immune to slights and
slanders and bitter persecution—indeed he knew more
than his share in the early years—and there is a strong

element of Negro nationalism in much of his work as well. See, for example, his novella "Bright and Morning Star," written in the thirties while he was still a Communist, where even the white Communists are suspect and untrustworthy. And it is interesting to note that his book about his Gold Coast experiences is called *Black Power* (1954)—a phrase that would become popular among American Negroes twelve years later.

Wright learned as a Negro living in the South that the rules, principles, and institutions of white America did not apply to him. And since he could not accept abject submission as a way of life, he endured a constant state of anxiety, and discovered the necessity of forging for himself his own ethics, his own morality, indeed his own personality, in a world that offered him little security or identity. This has since been called his "existentialism"— French existentialists after World War II seized upon Wright's works to support their own philosophy—but his views were formed long before he knew the meaning of the term.

Subsequent to the publication of *Native Son*, Wright was constantly asked by admirers and detractors alike how it was that he himself had not succumbed to the numbing docility of Southern Negroes. Wright was never quite able to answer satisfactorily, but there exist some clues in his autobiography, *Black Boy* (1945). Principally, one suspects, he was left to himself so much of the time in his early childhood, while his mother was away foraging for work, that he had to rely almost exclusively on his own inner resources simply to survive. Nor did the Wrights remain long enough in any one Negro community for Richard to pick up and assimilate the mores of defeatism. For the same reasons, he had little personal contact with the white world until his early adolescence—at which time his personality structure had already been formed. He was an outsider then not simply by being a Negro but by being a wanderer as well. Finally, he had the examples of his mother and various aunts and uncles, who were all at one time or another schoolteachers, and for whom some kind of learning must have made up a significant portion of their personalities. His principal defense against the anxieties that beset him were books, which he says he devoured with the voracity of an academician.

After the South, Wright moved to Chicago, where he lived until 1937. He worked at an odd assortment of jobs, and when the Depression struck, he suffered poverty even worse than he had known in Mississippi. His first fiction, a nondescript short story, was published in a Negro magazine in 1931, but he received considerable encouragement to continue with his writing at the Chicago John Reed Club, a radical organization devoted to the arts, which he joined in the early 1930's. It was here, Wright has said, working with white and Negro colleagues, that he discovered some of the most fulfilling experiences of his life. He joined the Communist Party in late 1933 and the Illinois Federal Writers' Project in 1935. Meanwhile he had begun publishing poems and stories—a few of them quite interesting—in left-wing periodicals and newspapers. In the summer of 1937 he moved to New York, and joined the staff of the *Daily Worker* as Harlem Editor. The following year he became a member of the New York Federal Writers' Project, where he wrote a scholarly and still highly informative essay on Harlem.

His first book, *Uncle Tom's Children,* four novellas depicting the lives of Southern Negroes, was published the same year, and in early 1940 his history-making *Native Son* was announced as a Book-of-the-Month-Club selection. Meanwhile, Wright had been collaborating with the photographer, Edwin Roskham, on a folk history of the American Negro. This was published in 1941 under the title *12 Million Black Voices,* to the plaudits of most reviewers. Wright's future seemed assured.

It is a paradox of Wright's success that he was returned to the initial anguish he had known in his Mississippi years. For some years he had been restive under Communist Party discipline, and his dissatisfaction grew considerably when, after the Nazi invasion of Russia, the Party seemingly abandoned the Negro cause in its all-out support of the American war effort. The final straw appears to have come when some of the Party leaders privately criticized *Native Son* as being ideologically incorrect. Wright did not break with the Party publicly until early 1942—and the decision was a difficult one to make. The Party had provided him with a sense of history and identity he had never known before—and now he was alone again in the American racist wilderness.

His works began to assume a more existential tone: a novella, "The Man Who Lived Underground" (1944), an eighteen-page introductory essay to Horace Cayton and St. Clair Drake's study of the Chicago Negro, *Black Metropolis* (1945), and an autobiography, *Black Boy* (1945). In 1946, a staunch admirer, Gertrude Stein, invited him to Paris, where French intellectuals met him with a hero's welcome and he was made an honorary citizen of France. The following year he moved permanently to Paris with his wife and child. He needed, he said, a race-free environment in which to carry out his work.

Wright's remaining years in Europe were not very productive of fiction. He wrote three more novels, two of which, *The Outsider* (1953) and *Savage Holiday* (1954), must be accounted artistic failures. His third novel, *The Long Dream* (1958), reveals a clearly marked resurgence of his powers. Wright's interests in this period, however, appear to have been more and more diverted to African and Asian nationalism. In 1948, he helped found, along with Sartre, Gide, Camus, and others, the periodical *Présence Africaine*, whose contents were largely devoted to articles, poems, and essays pertaining to Negro-American and African culture. He was also instrumental in establishing and promoting African cultural congresses that met in the fifties in Paris and Rome.

In 1953 he visited the Gold Coast at the invitation of Kwame Nkrumah, to observe the birth pangs of the first black African republic to be established since World War

II. Two years later, he attended the Afro-Asian Conference at Bandung as a reporter for the Congress of Cultural Freedom. His accounts of these events are recorded in *Black Power* (1954) and *The Color Curtain* (1956). In addition, he delivered a series of lectures throughout Europe dealing with the psychology and attitudes of colonial peoples. Some of these are compiled in *White Man, Listen!* (1957).

One of Wright's best journalistic efforts, however, did not relate at all to Asian and African problems, but rather to the psychology of the Spanish people some twenty-five years after their civil war. *Pagan Spain* (1957) was an intuitive and perceptive record of two trips he had made to Spain in late 1954 and the spring of 1955.

In the winter of 1960, Wright died of a heart attack, related in part to an amoebic disease he had contracted in Africa seven years earlier. He left behind him a wife and two daughters and a spirited controversy regarding his place in Negro American letters.

It would be fruitless to rehearse all the arguments for and against Wright. Generally, they center around the age-old question of the American expatriate—whether he hurts or helps his art by removing himself from his native soil. Perhaps even more acerbic have been the disputes regarding Wright's influence on future generations of Negro writers. A number of authors have paid homage to him, while James Baldwin and Ralph Ellison have publicly denied his influence, although both admit that Wright was instrumental in getting their initial works published. And yet Baldwin's angry voice and Ellison's existential themes are closely akin to Wright's works of the forties. Regardless of the merits of the controversy, there can be little question that *Native Son* opened up vistas of theme and subject matter that most Negro writers had previously avoided.

Native Son has as much impact now as it did when it was first published, in spite of the fact that its flaws are more obvious today than they could have been in the last years of the Depression, when proletarian literature still enjoyed a vogue. Nearly all the weaknesses and embarrassments we have come to recognize in proletarian fiction are present in *Native Son*, yet somehow the reader is not so conscious of them. One reason, of course, is that Bigger Thomas, unlike the usual array of proletarian victims, is thoroughly the antihero. (He is not simply weak, he is an outright coward. He is incapable of warmth, love, or loyalty, he is a sullen bully, and he enjoys his first sense of humanity and freedom only after he commits two brutal murders.)

Still, *Native Son* possesses many of the characteristic failings of proletarian literature. It is transparently propagandistic, arguing for a humane, socialist society where such crimes as Bigger committed could not conceivably take place. Wright builds up rather extensive documentation to prove that Bigger's actions, behavior, values, attitudes, and fate are determined by his status and place in American life. Bigger's immediate Negro environment is depicted as being unrelentingly bleak and empty, while the white world that stands just beyond his reach remains cruelly indifferent or hostile to his needs. With the exception of Bigger, none of the characters is portrayed in any depth, and most are depicted as representative "types" of the social class to which they belong. Despite his brutally conditioned psychology, there are moments in the novel when Bigger, like the heroes of other proletarian fiction, appears to be on the verge of responding to the stereotyped Communist vision of black and white workers marching together in the sunlight of fraternal friendship. Finally, Wright succumbs too often to the occupational disease of proletarian authors by hammering home sociological points in didactic expository prose when they could be understood just as clearly in terms of the organic development of the novel.

Yet if *Native Son* illustrates some of the conventional flaws of proletarian fiction, it also reveals Wright exploring new problems of character portrayal, prose style, and theme. As has already been suggested, there is the sympathetic presentation of perhaps one of the most disagreeable characters in fiction. And although *Native Son* makes its obvious sociological points, for well over two thirds of the novel Wright dwells on the peculiar states of mind of his protagonist, Bigger, which exist somehow outside the realm of social classes or racial issues. Indeed, Wright himself frequently makes the point that Bigger hangs psychologically suspended somewhere between the white world and the black.

> He felt he had no physical existence at all right then; he was something he hated, the badge of shame which he knew was attached to a black skin. It was a shadowy region, a No Man's Land, the ground that separated the white world from the black that he stood upon. He felt naked, transparent. . . .

Hence if categorizing terms are to be used, *Native Son* is as much a psychological novel as it is sociological, with Wright dwelling on various intensities of shame, fear and hate. Finally, there is the style. Since the viewpoint throughout is that of the illiterate and inarticulate Bigger, Wright had to discover a means of communicating thoughts and feelings Bigger is unable to express. At times Wright frankly interprets them to his readers, but often he reveals them in objectified images of Bigger's environment—the way the streets look to him, the feel of the sleet and the snow against his skin, the sounds of a rat rustling in the darkness of a tenement—and in dispassionate, unadorned accounts of Bigger's movements which in themselves give an accurate picture of Bigger's emotions.

To make his readers identify with the violent emotions and behavior of an illiterate Negro boy is no mean feat—but Wright goes beyond the mere shock of reader recognition, and the subsequent implications of shared guilt and social responsibility, and raises questions regarding the ultimate nature of man. What are man's responsibilities in a world devoid of meaning and purpose? That Wright couched these questions in what one critic has called the "linguistics" of Marxism has perhaps deterred readers from examining *Native Son* in the light of its other philosophical values. Since moral responsibility involves choice, can Wright's deterministic Marxism be reconciled with the freedom of action that choice implies? The contradiction is never resolved, and it is precisely for this reason that the novel fails to fulfill itself, for the plot, the structure, even the portrayal of Bigger himself, are often at odds with Wright's official determinism. But when on occasion the novel transcends its Marxist and proletarian limitations the reading becomes magnificent.

The structure of *Native Son* is classically simple. The book divides into three parts, the first two covering a little less than seventy-two hours, the third perhaps a little more than a month.

Book I, "Fear," traces a day in the life of twenty-year-old Bigger Thomas, from the time he wakes up in the morning and kills a rat in the squalid one room tenement he shares with his mother, sister, and brother, to the time he creeps back into bed twenty-one hours later, having just murdered a white girl. Bigger's day thus symbolically begins and ends in death. But Wright shows that all of Bigger's waking existence is a kind of meaninglessness—a kind of death. In the morning Bigger loiters on the street with members of his gang and plots (fearfully) to rob a white man's store. Later he goes to a movie and sits through a banal Hollywood double bill. Wright here shows how the glitter of the great white world beyond titillates Bigger and, at the same time, frustrates him all the more. When Bigger returns from the movie he has a savage fight in a pool room with one of the co-conspirators in the proposed robbery. Next he goes off to a job interview that has been arranged for him by the relief authorities. Mr. Dalton, the prospective employer, is a rich white man philanthropically inclined toward Negroes. He also owns considerable real estate in Chicago's South Side and

has a controlling interest in the house in which Bigger's
family lives. Bigger is hired as a chauffeur, and his first
assignment is to drive Dalton's daughter, Mary, to the
University. Once in the car, however, Mary redirects
Bigger to another address where she is joined by her
lover, Jan. Mary and Jan are Communists and want to
befriend Bigger; they sit up front with him in the car and
ask all sorts of intimate questions to which Bigger reacts
with suspicion and fear. It is women like Mary, he reasons, who have made things hard for Negroes. They make
Bigger take them to a Negro restaurant where they em-
barrass him by forcing him to join them at a table. Later
Bigger drives them around the park while Mary and Jan
drink from a bottle and make love in the back seat. After
Jan leaves, Bigger discovers Mary is much too drunk to
walk to the house by herself, so he carries her to her
bedroom and places her on the bed. He finds himself
somewhat sexually stimulated, but just at that moment
Mary's blind mother enters the room and calls to her
daughter. Bigger, fearing what Mrs. Dalton will think,
places a pillow over Mary's head so that she cannot respond. After Mrs. Dalton leaves, Bigger discovers he has
accidentally smothered Mary to death. He throws the
corpse into a trunk and takes the trunk downstairs to the
cellar where he thrusts Mary's body into the furnace. Then
he carries the trunk out to the car, since Mary had said she
wanted him to take it to the railroad station the following
morning. Thus ends Bigger's day—he goes home.

Wright forecasts Bigger's doom from the very start.
Bigger knows deep in his heart that he is destined to bear
endless days of dreary poverty, adject humiliation, and
tormenting frustration, for this is what being a Negro
means. Yet should he admit these things to himself, he
may well commit an act of unconscionable violence. "He
knew that the moment he allowed what his life meant to
enter fully into his consciousness, he would either kill
himself or someone else." And he knows he will not always be able to delude himself. He tells his friend, Gus,

early in the novel, "Sometimes I feel like something awful's going to happen to me." Hence, Bigger's principal fear is self-knowledge—and this, of course, is the theme and title of Book I. The other fears that make up Bigger's life are by-products of this basic terror.

All Bigger's actions stem from his fear. He hates whites because he fears them. He knows they are responsible for his immobility, his frustration, yet to admit even this would be admitting simultaneously a profound self-hatred. So he channels his hatred and aggression toward other Negroes, and thereby, momentarily at least, assuages his ego. He is afraid, for example, to steal from a white store keeper, and terrified that his friends can read his heart—so he attacks them in order to prove his courage to himself. He hates Mary Dalton because he fears she will jeopardize his job, and he regards all her overtures as efforts to humiliate him. He kills her because he fears the help he has given her will be misunderstood. Bigger's nature, then, is composed of dread and hate. He hates what he fears—and his bravado and violence are merely illusory compensations for his terror.

The second book, "Flight," describes Bigger's awakening sense of life at a time, paradoxically, when his life is most in danger. Although his killing of Mary was an accident, Bigger decides that he must assume full responsibility for her death. Hence, for once in his life he will know the consequences of an action he has "voluntarily" taken. In killing Mary, he feels, he has destroyed symbolically all the oppressive forces that have made his life a misery. Thus perhaps her death was not so accidental as it seemed at the time. He enjoys a sense of potency and freedom that he has never before experienced. He knows something, has done something, that the whites do not know—and proceeds now to act with new-found dignity. Ironically the dignity takes the form of acts compounding his crime. He plans to lay the blame for Mary's disappearance on Jan. Jan was, after all, the last white person to see Mary alone; he is also a Communist, and Bigger knows most Communists are hated. He succeeds in implying Jan's guilt and Jan is arrested and held for questioning. Meanwhile Bigger has revealed to his girl, Bessie, that he is involved in Mary's disappearance—which is now front page news—and Bessie reluctantly agrees to help him extort ransom from the Daltons under the pretense that their daughter has been kidnaped. This plan falls through when reporters discover Mary's charred bones in the furnace, and Bigger is forced to flee. He and Bessie conceal themselves in a vacated tenement, but Bigger realizes Bessie is at best an unenthusiastic co-conspirator, and decides he must kill her or she will some day reveal his whereabouts to the police. He makes love to her and after she has gone to sleep he smashes her head in with a brick. The monstrousness of the second murder exhilarates Bigger all the more:

> And, yet, out of it all, over and above all that had happened, impalpable but real, there remained to him a queer sense of power. *He* had done this. *He* had brought all this about. In all his life these two murders were the most meaningful things that had ever happened to him. He was living, truly and deeply, no matter what others might think, looking at him with their blind eyes. Never had he had the chance to live out the consequence of his actions; never had his will been so free as in this night and day of fear and murder and flight.

Hence Bigger has *opted* to become a murderer, and freely chosen this identity. In an absurd, hostile world that denies his humanity and dichotomizes his personality, he has made a choice that somehow integrates his being:

> There was something he *knew* and something he *felt;* something the *world* gave him and something he *himself* had; something spread out in *front* of him and something spread out in *back;* and never in all his life, with this black skin of his, had the two worlds, thought and feeling, will and mind, aspiration and satisfaction, been together; never had he felt a sense of wholeness.

· · · · · · · · · · · · · ·

He had committed murder twice and had created a new world for himself.

Ironically, Bigger has assumed exactly the role the white world thrusts upon the Negro in order to justify his oppression. If the Negro is a beast who must be caged in order to protect the purity of the white race, that is at least an identity—preferable to that of someone obsequious, passive, and happily acquiescent to his exploitation. Bigger's choices are moral and metaphysical, not political or racial. He has the choice, as Esther Merle Jackson has pointed out, between force and submission, love and hate, life and death. He elects force as a sign of his being, and by rebelling against established authority—despite the impossibility of success—he acquires a measure of freedom.

None of the above is intended to deny that oppressive environmental factors limit the modes of Bigger's actions; nonetheless, environment by itself does not explain Bigger. Bigger's original alienation from the Negro community was made of his own free choice. His mother, his sister, his girl—each has made an individual adjustment of some sort to the conditions of Negro life. But Bigger cannot accept his mother's religiosity, his sister's Y.W.C.A. virtue, or Bessie's whisky. All seem to him evasions of reality. Though his rejection of Negro life was only a negative choice, his acts of murder are positive—thus in a degree humanizing—since he is quite prepared to accept the consequences.

The remainder of Book II has a taut, tense rhythm corresponding to the quickening pace of flight and pursuit. As the police inexorably close in, Bigger flies from one street to the next, one tenement to the next; he is chased across roofs—until finally he is flung down from the chimney to which he has been clinging by the pressure of the water directed at him from the hoses of firemen.

Book III, "Fate," draws together all the significant strands of Bigger's life, and shows how all society, white and black, has a stake in his crimes. The newspapers, the police, and the politicians use Bigger for their own self-aggrandizement. The Communists defend him, although even they do not altogether understand him. Futile attempts are made to convert him to Christianity. Philanthropists and the business community are implicated, since both are exploiters of the Negro. Racists burn crosses in various parts of the city; outside the courtroom in which Bigger is tried, a howling white mob cries for his blood. Bigger's attorney, Max, in a useless but eloquent address to the jury, tries to explain Bigger's crimes in terms of the devastating psychological blows of slavery and racial exploitation.

Immediately after his capture, Bigger reverts to his pose of sullen apathy. But Max's genuine efforts to help and understand him awaken in Bigger a vague sense of hope and trust in men. He needs Max and looks forward to his visits. He knows the jury will doom him, but this does not disturb him very much. Throughout the agony of his trial, Bigger has been trying to puzzle through the meaning of his life and world. He has always lived so isolated from other human beings that he is no longer sure. He asks Max, but even Max can only respond in historical and socioeconomic terms. Some day, Max tells him, men might be able to express their beings in terms other than struggle and exploitation. But although moved, Bigger cannot ultimately accept this. For him the essence of life is violence and power.

> "I didn't want to kill!" Bigger shouted. "But what I killed for, I *am!* . . . What I killed for must have been good!" Bigger's voice was full of frenzied anguish. "It must have been good! When a man kills, it's for something. . . . I didn't know I was really alive in this world until I felt things hard enough to kill for 'em. . . ."

Bigger elects to face death on the same principles that have finally made his life meaningful.

The chief philosophical weakness of *Native Son* is not that Bigger does not surrender his freedom to Max's de-

terminism, or that Bigger's Zarathustrian principles do
not jibe with Max's socialist visions; it is that Wright
himself does not seem to be able to make up his mind.
The reader feels that Wright, although intellectually
committed to Max's views, is more emotionally akin to
Bigger's. And somehow Bigger's impassioned hatred
comes across more vividly than Max's eloquent reasoning.
Indeed, the very length of Max's plea to the jury (sixteen
pages in the Harper edition) suggests that Wright,
through Max, is endeavoring to convince himself.

The whole of Book III seems out of key with the first
two-thirds of the novel. Where Books I and II confine
themselves to a realistic account of Bigger's thoughts and
actions, Book III tries to interpret these in a number of
rather dubious symbolic sequences. In one scene Bigger,
in his cell, confronts all the people with whom he has
previously been involved: the Daltons, Jan, a Negro
preacher, his mother, brother, and sister, three members
of his street gang, Max, and the district attorney. Everything is highly contrived—as if Wright is placing before
Bigger's eyes all the major influences that have made up
his life. In another scene of transparently "symbolic" significance, Bigger, after a trying day in court, flings a
wooden crucifix out of the cell door, thereby suggesting
his rejection of Christianity.

Perhaps the most flagrant violation of verisimilitude is
Max's plea to the jury. Although it undoubtedly makes
good sociological sense and is possibly even a sound assessment of Bigger's character, it is not the sort of thing
that would ordinarily persuade a jury. A more realistic
approach to the intensely hysterical courtroom atmosphere would have been for Max to plead some sort of
insanity—rather than to depict Bigger as a helpless victim
of American civilization.

Finally, Book III contains a number of improbable
colloquies between Bigger and Max. Here Bigger is almost unbelievable. After twenty years of conditioning to
mistrust every human being, especially whites, he sud-

denly opens up and bares his soul to Max. The point Wright is making is a good one: no one has ever before cared to understand Bigger as a human being and not as a symbol; no one has ever before granted him his dignity. Nonetheless, to suggest that Bigger would respond so quickly to Max, under such circumstances, is to make excessive demands on the credulity of the reader.

The inconsistency of Wright's ideologies and philosophical attitudes prevents Bigger and the other characters from developing properly, adulterates the structure of the novel, and occasionally clouds an otherwise lucid prose style.

There are three kinds of revolutionism in *Native Son*— and none of them altogether engages the reader as representing Wright's point of view. Max's communism is of course what Wright presumes his novel is expressing—yet this kind of revolutionism is, as we have seen, imposed from without and not an integral element of Bigger's being. Revolutionism of a Negro nationalist variety is far more in keeping with Bigger's character. Bigger hates all whites with such an intensity that it gives him extreme pleasure to think he killed Mary deliberately. His is a reverse racism. As Max puts it:

> Every time he comes in contact with us, he kills! It is a physiological and psychological reaction, embedded in his being. Every thought he thinks is potential murder. Excluded from, and unassimilated in our society, yet longing to gratify impulses akin to our own . . . every sunrise and sunset make him guilty of subversive actions. Every movement of his body is an unconscious protest. Every desire, every dream, no matter how intimate or personal, is a plot or a conspiracy. Every hope is a plan for insurrection. Every glance of the eye is a threat. *His very existence is a crime against the state!*

Sometimes Bigger's racism takes more of a political form:

> There were rare moments when a feeling and longing for solidarity with other black people would take hold of

him. He would dream of making a stand against that white
force. . . . He felt that some day there would be a black
man who would whip the black people into a tight band
and together they would act. . . .

But as Camus has written, "Human rebellion ends in
metaphysical revolution"—and it is in the role of the
metaphysical revolutionary that Bigger looms most significantly for modern readers. The metaphysical revolutionary challenges the very conditions of being—the needless
suffering, the absurd contrast between his inborn sense of
justice and the amorality and injustice of the external
world. He tries to bring the world into accord with his
sense of justice, but if this fails he will attempt to match
in himself its injustice and chaos. In either case the prin-
ciple is the same: "He attacks a shattered world in order
to demand unity from it."

In *How Bigger Was Born* (a piece Wright produced
afterward, describing the genesis of the novel), Wright
describes it thus:

> [It was] a world whose fundamental assumptions could
> no longer be taken for granted, a world ridden with class
> and national strife, a world whose metaphysical meanings
> had vanished . . . a world in which men could no longer
> retain their faith in an ultimate hereafter.

By rejecting these "fundamental assumptions" and identifying himself with the world of violence and strife he
knows to be true, Bigger gives his life meaning and clarity:

> He felt that he had his destiny in his grasp. He was
> more alive than he could ever remember having been; his
> mind and attention were pointed, focused toward a goal.
> For the first time in his life he moved consciously between
> two sharply defined poles: he was moving away from the
> threatening penalty of death, from the death-like times
> that brought him that tightness and hotness in his chest;
> and he was moving toward that sense of fullness. . . .

Compare Camus's description of the romantic criminal,
Satan:

Since violence is at the root of all creation, deliberate violence shall be its answer. The fact that there is an excess of despair adds to the causes of despair and brings rebellion to that state of indignant frustration which follows the long experience of injustice and where the distinction between good and evil finally disappears.

Perhaps it is Bigger's Satanic election of violence, rather than his continued undying hatred of whites, that so terrifies Max at the close of the novel. Max senses that as a Communist he too has dispensed with the old social order—but the metaphysical vacuum that has been created does not necessarily lead men like Bigger to communism; it may just as easily lead to the most murderous kind of nihilism. Max's horror was to become Wright's own dilemma two years after the publication of *Native Son*, when he himself left the Party. He could no longer accept the assumptions of communism, yet the prospects of a new world of positive meaning and value seemed very distant indeed. It is, then, in the roles of a Negro nationalist revolutionary and a metaphysical rebel that Wright most successfully portrays Bigger. And it is from these aspects of Bigger's character rather than from any Marxist interpretation that Wright's sociology really emerges.

The metaphor that Wright uses best to illustrate the relationship between the races is "blindness"—and blindness is one result of Bigger's racist nationalist pride. Prior to his conversion by murder, Bigger has blinded himself to the realities of Negro life (as well as to the humanity of whites—he is unable to accept Jan's offer of friendship, for example, because he blindly regards all whites as symbols of oppression). It is only after his metaphysical rebellion has been effected by the death of the two girls that Bigger acquires sight. When he looks at his family, he realizes they are as blind as he had been; he understands what it means to be a Negro. Buddy, his brother, "was blind . . . Buddy, too, went round and round in a groove and did not see things. Buddy's clothes hung loosely compared with the way Jan's hung. Buddy seemed aimless,

lost, with no sharp or hard edges, like a chubby puppy . . .
he saw in Buddy a certain stillness, an isolation, meaninglessness." When he looks at his mother he sees "how soft
and shapeless she was. . . . She moved about slowly,
touching objects with her fingers as she passed them,
using them for support. . . . There was in her heart, it
seemed, a heavy and delicately balanced burden whose
weight she did not want to assume by disturbing it one
whit." His sister, Vera, "seemed to be shrinking from life
in every gesture she made. The very manner in which she
sat showed a fear so deep as to be an organic part of her.
. . ."

Bigger's new vision also enables him to see how blind
whites are to his humanity, his existence. Whites prefer to
think of Negroes in easily stereotyped images of brute
beast or happy minstrel. They are incapable of viewing
black men as possessing sensitivity and intelligence. It is
this blindness that Bigger counts on as the means of getting away with his crimes. When he schemes with Bessie
to collect ransom money from the Daltons, he tells her:
"They think the Reds is doing it. They won't think *we*
did. They don't think we got enough guts to do it. They
think niggers is too scared. . . ." Even well-meaning people like Mr. and Mrs. Dalton are blind to the sufferings of
Negroes. Believing that acts of charity can somehow
miraculously banish in Negroes feelings of shame, fear,
and suspicion, the Daltons lavish millions of dollars on
Negro colleges and welfare organizations—while at the
same time they continue to support the rigid caste system
that is responsible for the Negroes' degradation in the first
place. Mrs. Dalton's blindness is symbolic of the blindness of the white liberal philanthropic community.

Finally, the Communists, Mary, Jan, and Max, are just
as blind to the humanity of Negroes as the others—even
though they presumably want to enlist Negroes as equals
in their own cause. For Mary and Jan, Bigger is an ab-
straction—a symbol of exploitation rather than someone
whose feelings they have ever really tried to understand.

Although he does not know it, this is really the reason Bigger hates them. Even when Mary concedes her blindness she has no idea how condescending her statements sound:

> "You know, Bigger, I've long wanted to go into those houses," she said, pointing to the tall, dark apartment buildings looming to either side of them, "and just *see* how your people live. You know what I mean? I've been to England, France and Mexico, but I don't know how people live ten blocks from me. We know so *little* about each other. I just want to *see*. I want to *know* these people. Never in my life have I been inside of a Negro home. Yet they *must* live like we live. They're human. . . . There are twelve million of them. . . . They live in our country. . . . In the same city with us. . . ." her voice trailed off wistfully.

In the final analysis, *Native Son* stands on shifting artistic grounds. Had Wright only managed to affix a different ending, more in accord with the character of Bigger and the philosophical viewpoint he seeks to embody, the novel might have emerged a minor masterpiece. Yet, for all its faults, *Native Son* retains surprising power. The reasons are still not clearly understood, even by present-day critics.

It is not simply that the "Negro problem" has once more intruded itself onto the national consciousness, if not the national conscience—although "sociology" should certainly not be discounted as an important factor. Nor is it merely the sensational nature of the crimes Bigger committed, compounded as they were with racial and sexual overtones. In part, of course, it is the terrible excitement, the excruciating suspense of flight and pursuit that Wright invests in his best prose. In part, too, it is the shock of unembellished hatred in Wright's portrayal of a seemingly nondescript, apathetic Negro boy.

James Baldwin, writing of *Native Son*, says every Negro carries about within him a Bigger Thomas—but that the characterization by itself is unfair in that there are complexities, depths to the Negro psychology and life, that Wright has left unexplored. To depict Bigger exclusively in terms of unsullied rage and hatred is to do the Negro a disservice. In Baldwin's view, Bigger is a "monster."

This, of course, is precisely the point Wright wishes to make—and herein lies its most terrible truth for the reader. Wright is obviously not describing the "representative" Negro—although he makes clear that what has happened to Bigger can more easily befall Negroes than whites. He is describing a person so alienated from traditional values, restraints, and civilized modes of behavior, that he feels free to construct his own ethics—that for him an act of murder is an act of creation.

But can such a person exist? Yes, if his actual experiences contradict the interpretations that civilization ordinarily puts on human action. Although Bigger dreams the American dreams, he knows he can never realize them because he is a Negro. If the civilization rejects him out of hand, he will reject the traditional and acceptable means and values for achieving the rewards that civilization has to offer. This is not a conscious rationalizing process on the part of Bigger—it is almost second nature. How else can he do more than survive? Such "monsters," as Baldwin calls them, exist. Our tabloids could not exist without them. But even supposing they do not commit murder, their sense of isolation and alienation is growing in the face of an increasingly impersonal mass society. And in mass, the isolated, the alienated, are capable of consent or indifference to napalm bombs, nuclear holocaust, or extermination camps.

It is perhaps in this respect that Native Son is so much more disturbing today than when it was first published. It is not that Bigger Thomas is so different from us; it is that he is so much like us.

Chapter V

Race and Sex:
The Novels of Chester Himes

Chester Himes is one of the most prolific of all Negro novelists. At this writing, he is the author of six major novels and a number of lively potboilers about a couple of Harlem detectives. Although he enjoys a good reputation in France, where he now lives, for the most part the American critics have dismissed him as being of the Wright school of naturalism, whose "protest" is no longer fashionable. Such criticism is not altogether fair. Himes's interests are considerably different from Wright's, and his firsthand knowledge of certain areas of American life is more developed. His protagonists are generally middle-class, fairly well-educated, somewhat sophisticated in the ways of the world, and often intellectually oriented. They are concerned with ideas and the application of ideas to their experience; they are constantly searching out rational explanations for the irrationalities of their lives. They move with considerable aplomb among white liberals and radicals of both sexes, and engage them in dialectics on their own terms. Himes is also a more deliberate prose stylist than Wright. He seldom intrudes, moralizes, or explains. His characters are usually sufficiently articulate to say what they mean—and what they mean issues often enough from their character and intelligence. Himes does parallel Wright in his bitterness, fury, and frustration. He has given up on America, and rarely returns now on visits.

In an autobiographical novel, *The Third Generation* (1954), Himes relates the growth into young manhood of Charles Taylor, the son of genteel, decorous Southern parents. Charles grows up in Cleveland, attends public school with white children, and spends some time at Ohio State University. As the novel progresses, Charles and his family disintegrate under the pressures of modern urban life and of the insidious racism that underlies their social and familial relationships.

Although generally well-written, the novel is more interesting as a psychological study than as a finished work of fiction, since Himes never really focuses in on his theme. He does, however, very delicately and compassionately attempt to understand his characters. On the surface, rank bigotry seldom intrudes as the direct cause of their suffering; they appear to be defeated by their own incapacities, weaknesses, blindness, and obsessions. But Himes makes clear that in order to understand them, one must understand the generations that preceded them, black and white: they are doomed not simply by their own psychic drives but by the history that created them and forced them into self-destructive channels. They are as much the victims of a value system they implicitly accept (and which indeed flows in their bloodstreams) as are men like Bigger Thomas who rebel against the social order.

Himes feels the trunk and roots of American society are so corrupted as to make normal growth and development impossible. His concern is not primarily with social protest, as has so often been alleged, for protest implies some hope of appropriate reform, and Himes, one suspects, regards the American scene as beyond redemption. His principal subject is the human consequences of a distorted and diseased civilization. His characters, on the other hand, prefer to interpret their warped and maddened psyches in terms of the society that has conditioned them. Being Negroes, they are more attuned to social abuse, and being middle-class or intellectual, they are all the more aware of their frustrations since their aspirations, though similar to those of the white bourgeoisie, are blocked by their color. "Successful" professional Negroes are frequently more embittered than persons of lower socioeconomic strata, whose expectations are not nearly so great. And it is men like Himes who are often the bitterest enemies of their own social class for having compromised their values in submission to caste mores.

Somewhere James Baldwin has written that Chester Himes is the only Negro writer who has described male-female relationships in other than violent terms. This is not altogether accurate, since Jessie Fauset and Nella Larsen probed along these lines in the 1920's, as have some latter-day novelists, notably Kristin Hunter and Paule Marshall. Nor is Himes's treatment of love without its elements of sadism and self-laceration. But it is undoubtedly true that Himes, in each of his major works, has focused much of his attention on lovers, and has attempted to track down the vagaries and nuances of their emotions. He has, in addition, an unabashed eye for the physical and sensual. It is true as well that he appears to be devoting more and more of his work to material hitherto regarded as taboo—interracial love. Perhaps Himes feels, like so many other Negro authors and intellectuals, that underlying the structure of American society is an unresolved residue of erotic racial guilt that manifests itself, among other ways, as "the Negro problem."

Himes's first novel, *If He Hollers Let Him Go* (1945), is related in the first person, in hard-boiled, Hemingway-esque prose, by a young Negro who works in a Los Angeles shipyard during World War II. In the course of the novel, Bob Jones loses his girl, is demoted in his job, becomes involved in a brawl in which he is unjustly accused of attempted rape, and ultimately promises to enlist in order to avoid imprisonment. But his declining fortune is forecast in the first pages of the novel by a near paranoid state of mind—and in that sense there is no real progression in the novel. Everything that happens to Bob —and there are humiliations, rebuffs and insults from beginning to end—only serves to justify the extremity of his emotions. Had Himes shown Jones to be more trusting from the start, the effect might be cumulative rather than tedious.

What intrigues the reader, however, is not what his first novel might have been, but rather his discovery of the themes that he would employ to greater advantage later on. This is a race novel in the purest sense of the term. Bob's tensions are produced and aggravated by the bigotry he meets everywhere. He lives from one moment to the next on the edge of violence, terrified not only of what others may do to him, but of what he feels about himself. Specifically, systematic racism has awakened in him deep castration fears—has indeed psychologically emasculated him, robbing him of his self-esteem since he is constantly being reminded of his "place" in the scheme of things. In compensation, Bob drives his car furiously, drinks hard, fights hard, and makes love to the wife of one of his friends. But his principal torment is that he is intellectually aware of what is happening to him, but cannot muster sufficient strength to save himself as he watches his fate overtake him.

His dreams of crippled men and tethered dogs describe to him metaphorically the realities of his waking condition.

> The alarm went off again. . . . I groped for it blindly, shut it off; I kept my eyes shut tight. But I began feeling

scared in spite of hiding from the day. It came along with
consciousness. It came into my head first, somewhere back
of my closed eyes, moving slowly underneath my skull to
the base of my brain, cold and hollow. It seeped down
my spine, into my arms, spread through my groin with an
almost sexual torture, settled in my stomach like butterfly
wings. For a moment I felt torn all loose inside, shriveled,
paralyzed, as if after a while I'd have to get up and die.

Bob himself never employs clinical language to explain
the erotic implications of the psychosocial roles he knows
he plays—but the meaning is never far from the surface.
Not only does white society emasculate him, but it tends
simultaneously to regard him as an envied symbol of sexual strength from which white women must be protected.
Implicit here is Himes's view that the sexual insecurity of
the white American male impels him to suppress the
Negro in order to bolster his shaky masculine ego. Other
Negro authors—Wright and Baldwin especially—have
played variations on this same theme. In their view the
Negro represents the objectification of the white man's
antisocial libidinal fancies. In suppressing the Negro, the
white man attempts to suppress what he most fears about
himself.

In his next novel, *Lonely Crusade* (1947), Himes ex-
tends the fantasy one step further to the white woman.
The white mistress of a Negro man often unknowingly
experiences feelings of smug *noblesse oblige* in giving herself to an "inferior." At critical moments, however, she
will retreat behind caste barriers rather than risk social
disapproval. Lee Gordon, for example, learns that his
white mistress will not condescend to fight over him with
his wife—not out of tender considerations for his family
life, but because it would offend her sense of racial superiority to squabble with a Negro woman. The white
woman finds the Negro eminently desirable as the forbid-
den embodiment of her sexual yearnings; on the other
hand, he also stands for her guilt and shame about these
feelings. She punishes herself by taking the Negro at the
same time that she gratifies herself physically. Or should

she be rebelling against social conventions, she may use
the Negro as a symbol of her defiance. Whatever the com-
bination of motives, in no case is the Negro's essential
humanity recognized. Rather do white and Negro lovers
play games with one another, using one another as objects
of wish fulfillment.

Lonely Crusade is a sprawling, uneven novel of ideas
dealing with the life of an uncommitted West Coast Negro
union organizer, Lee Gordon, who after a series of mis-
haps learns to overcome his deep-seated caste-conditioned
fears and suspicions and achieve a sense of identity.
There are lengthy passages relating to dialectical materialism, anti-Semitism among Negroes, and Negro attitudes
toward labor unions—and some of these have a certain
intrinsic value. Moreover, Himes has been able to create a
few authentic characters who manage to stand out in vivid
contrast to a somewhat strained, at times oversentimentalized plot.

But Himes is really at his best in portraying Lee Gordon's relationships to his wife and mistress. He shows the
gradual deterioration of a marriage as Lee Gordon discovers his wife is better able to provide for herself than
he. Conversely, he shows how Lee temporarily regains an
illusion of manhood with a white woman whose demands
are primarily sexual. The emasculating effects of racism
are again the deepest source of Lee's misery, and Himes
traces these in graphic emotional detail. But the story
resolves itself in a strange upbeat ending (resembling the
proletarian novel of the thirties), in which Lee decides he
cannot blame race for everything and throws in his lot
with the struggling working man for the betterment of
white and Negro alike.

The novel is thus clearly derivative, but Himes's insights are good, particularly as regards the Negro's attraction to the white woman. On the most obvious level, she
is an object of fear, since any suspicions of interracial
sex may lead to death and castration. When Lee Gordon,
as a young boy, is discovered hiding in a girls' locker

room, he and his family scurry out of town in order to avoid possible ghastly consequences. Yet because of the mysterious taboo aura with which she is endowed, Himes's Negro men find the white woman all the more desirable. This desire is often mixed with hate, since she is viewed as the original cause of their pariah status; moreover, possessing a white woman may serve as an act of clandestine revenge on the white man who persecutes them. Finally, the white woman may provide the Negro with the sense of masculinity which he fails to achieve with women of his own race. In a society where the man is expected to support and protect his women, the Negro male who finds himself unable to do so for caste and economic reasons may turn for solace to the white woman.*

In the development of the novel, Lee Gordon does just this. The presence of his wife, who earns more money than he, serves as a constant reminder of his shame. He directs the anger he feels about himself toward her, and she loses respect for him as a man. Recriminations feed upon one another and the effects on the marriage are corrosive. Yet the respite Lee finds with a white woman is at best illusory. He can only feel himself equal to her, he says, when he pities her. Thus does race consciousness cast a pall over lovers.

On the surface, *The Primitive* (1955), appears to be far less ambitious than Himes's previous undertakings. For one thing, he narrows his scope considerably, focusing on two rather atypical characters and their circle of estranged Bohemian acquaintances. The setting of the novel alternates between a shabby Harlem tenement and a

---

* In a study, *Mark of Oppression*, published in 1951, psychologists Abram Kardiner and Lionel Ovesey suggest that the relatively high desertion rate among husbands of Negro lower-class families may be understood in terms similar to those Himes describes. According to the authors, when the Negro husband feels that his role in the family structure has been undermined as a result of his inability to provide financial support, he may choose to leave home rather than face the emotional consequences of his failure.

Gramercy Park apartment, lending the story a kind of
staged theatrical quality. Finally, the concentrated time
span—six days—within which the narrative is encom-
passed, forcibly limits the range of action of its participants. The novel does, nonetheless, explore many of the
same problems as his previous works and represents
Himes's best artistic effort to date.

The two major characters are an unsuccessful Negro
novelist, Jesse, and a white woman, Kriss, who holds a
responsible administrative position at a Madison Avenue
foundation called the India Institute. The first few chapters alternate between Kriss and Jesse—Kriss in her
apartment, at her job, and among friends; Jesse in the
dreary Harlem rooms that he shares with disreputable
tenants, or out on the streets wandering aimlessly from
one bar to the next. They meet, having not seen each
other for several years, and each uses the other for his
own neurotic needs. The latter portion of the novel describes a week-end drinking party at Kriss's house, where
Kriss and Jesse are visited by a number of "liberal" intellectual friends, white and Negro. The presence of these
exacerbates their feelings of defeat and failure, and each
turns on the other with increased hate and venom. Jesse
apparently kills Kriss in a state of drunken oblivion (the
scene is not described but alluded to after the event), and
the novel closes on Jesse calling the police to inform them
of her death.

Himes endeavors to relate their own emotional chaos
to corresponding absurdities in world affairs. From time
to time Kriss tunes in a television interview with a chim-
panzee who can predict the news. The monkey responds to
specific questions by reciting news dispatches that will be
broadcast at some future date. The effectiveness of this
device is somewhat compromised by the fact that Jesse
and Kriss provide no suitable reference point of sanity.
Their imbalance appears too much the product of their
own peculiar backgrounds, so it remains for the reader to
link up the madness within and the madness without.

It is not that Himes has not made the effort. He traces their history in terms of the environment that has fashioned them. Kriss was brought up in North Dakota, the only daughter of an alcoholic German nobleman and a mother of Scandinavian peasant stock. When she was sixteen, she was seduced, and the abortion that followed rendered her sterile. Later she works in Chicago as an assistant to a Negro sociologist researching race relations. The interracial, Bohemian group with whom she associated during this period pressured her into marrying a white Mississippian, who turned out to be a homosexual. Her numerous subsequent liaisons with men of both races were an attempt to compensate for the terrifying hurt and loneliness she had felt all her life. When she meets Jesse again in New York (they had last shared alcoholic moments together in an artists' colony), she is divorced and has just been rejected by a man she had hoped to marry. On the surface Kriss appears to be a very elegant and successful career woman, but in truth she is despairing and hysterical, and uses drink and promiscuity to stave off her loneliness. Kriss is a well-realized character, but the extremities of her situation appear to have been induced by her environment only in the most general way. Rather does she seem to be the victim of chance circumstances and a certain central weakness of character. She is not a racist, but she does resort to racial fantasies to compensate for feelings of inadequacy, and she uses the racial fears of her white and Negro lovers to exact her revenge on men—on whom, usually, she places the blame for her psychological undoing. Nor is she a racial "radical" advocating miscegenation and free love as a social cure-all. Her dearest wish is to marry into the respectable white middle class and live a normal bourgeois life. To imagine Kriss as a reduced version of the absurdities she watches on television is somewhat far-fetched.

Jesse, on the other hand, is more understandable. His bitterness stems in part from the racial humiliation he has suffered all his life, in part from the fact that he cannot support his wife (and has, as a result, left her), and in part from the sordid conditions in which he lives. Jesse's third novel, on which he had been working for more than a year, has been turned down for publication. The reading public, he is told, is tired of protest; he should try writing novels with more "uplift." When Jesse observes that he can write only about the life he knows, he is advised to write about successful Negroes like himself.

Jesse and Kriss torture themselves for the causes of their misery. Jesse takes his rejected manuscript back to his room and plunges a knife through it. Kriss gets drunk and attempts suicide but fails when the sleeping pills spill out of her hand. But Jesse differs from Kriss in that he entertains no illusions about the attractions of the bourgeois life. He is always somewhat detached from himself and from his world. He is his own chorus character, cynically watching himself submerge, yet helpless to stop himself. He is a soured intellectual, destroyed as much by his passivity as by his mind.

When they meet again, their story becomes a dance of death wherein the black man and the white woman tease and taunt and thrust at one another until both are destroyed. Within this macabre framework, Himes projects varying degrees of alcoholic murk through which his two principals attempt to grope their way. On occasion, however, he will introduce flat documentary prose in order to keep his characters in some kind of touch with reality. Hence Jesse may awaken in his Harlem room from a drunken stupor and see the following items by his bedside:

> Beyond the ashtray was a half-emptied package of Camel cigarettes, a half-eaten, twenty-five-cent bar of milk chocolate, a half-emptied, pint-sized carton of milk, a small white enameled alarm clock with a broken crystal, and a milk-stained water glass smelling of gin. All were clustered like a repulsive brood of hybrids about a pumpkin-sized spherical bottle containing a green solution, which comprised the base of a night lamp which had a large faded

pink shade that sat loosely on a frame made for something else.

The title of the novel, *The Primitive*, of course refers to the role Jesse plays in his affair with Kriss. From the world's viewpoint Jesse lives up to this image by murdering Kriss. But the irony lies in the fact that, far from being primitive, Jesse kills because he is overcivilized. His sensibilities have been stretched to the breaking point, and it is precisely because he feels his individual humanity is never recognized that he finds his existence unbearable. In killing Kriss, Jesse strikes back at the primitivism of "civilized" whites who deny him his dignity. His "primitive" act of violence thus makes him civilized in their eyes. When he realizes he has murdered Kriss, he muses sardonically to himself that he can now join the human race.

Himes's point is basically that anything that dehumanizes is primitive, and the racial attitudes of American society are symptoms of a dehumanized culture. The India Institute, where Kriss works, is a case in point. Kriss's colleagues are passionless and petty, and although the Institute is presumably dedicated to humanitarian ends, none of the employees appears to find his work meaningful. The dehumanized lives of all Americans, from the exploited poor to the characterless sophisticates of Kriss's circle, torment Jesse in drunken dreams. Perhaps most symbolic of all is the prophetic monkey forecasting the news. It is as if this nonhuman, precivilized creature really expresses the nature of American life.

It is in the area of sexual relationships that the theme of the novel makes its greatest impact. Kriss and Jesse perceive one another in primitive images—not as individuals but as projections of their own inchoate impulses, desires, and terrors. For Kriss, Jesse is at once a symbol of sexual power, a whipping boy for all her self-loathing and frustration, and an instrument to taunt the sensibilities of white men who have rejected her in the past. But

Kriss, by a strange twist of logic, tends subconsciously to blame Negroes for the failure of her marriage. In taking a Negro lover, she can also direct her anger toward Negro men generally. For her, an act of love is as much an act of hostility as anything else. Jesse, in turn, is motivated by certain primitive and dangerous elements in his nature. When he first sees Kriss he feels himself utterly defeated; in a way he is already spiritually dead. Prior to their meeting he says he *needs a white woman*. Without acknowledging it to himself, Jesse is seeking out his physical destruction, but just as significantly he is seeking out the cause of his destruction. For him Kriss represents the white world that has crushed him, and, unconsciously, Jesse decides to kill her. Kriss knows of Jesse's intentions; she watches him sadistically as he writhes in his sleep, muttering to himself, "Kill you!" Yet she does not flee, for she seeks her own death. It would be her final act of vengeance on all the men who have drained her.

It is difficult to do justice to this novel. Parts are extremely well-written and Himes's cast of characters is authentically conceived. Jesse is especially interesting. His self-pity—of which he has plenty—is seldom irritating, and this is a remarkable feat for any author. Himes laces Jesse's gloom with a kind of dry wit, a sad intellectual humor that saves him from sentimentality.

No more worrying about what's right and what's wrong. Just what's expedient. You're human now. Went in the back door of the Alchemy Company of America a primitive, filled with things called principles, integrity, honor, conscience, faith, love, hope, charity and such, and came out the front door a human being, completely purged. End of a primitive; beginning of a human. Good title for a book but won't sell in America with the word *human* in it. Americans sensitive about that word. Don't want to know they're human. Don't blame them, though. Poses the only problem they've never been able to solve with all their gadgets—the human problem. But they'll know damn well you're human. Be in all the newspapers: *Black man kills white woman*. Not only natural, plausible,

logical, inevitable, psychiatrically compulsive and sociolog-
ically conclusive behavior of a human being, but mathe-
matically accurate and politically correct as well. Black
man has got to have some means of joining the human
race. Old Shakespeare knew. Suppose he'd had Othello
kiss the bitch and make up. Would have dehumanized
him.

This is Himes's most pessimistic work. He has lost
faith in the human capacity to reason its way out of its
dilemmas. Jesse and Kriss, two intelligent human beings,
are as muddled and distressed about their own identities
as the worst racists. But here lies the trouble. Himes has,
in a curious way, written two books—one about Jesse and
Kriss, and one about racist America—and the two do not
quite mesh, because Jesse and Kriss are too atypical and
too idiosyncratic. Himes's ideas require a novel with a
wider scope than one shabby Harlem tenement, one
Gramercy Park apartment, and a few decadent intellectuals. Whether or not he will succeed in writing such a
novel remains to be seen.

Himes's latest work on similar subject matter is a broad
comic farce, *Pinktoes* (1965). Ironically, *Pinktoes*, the
least of Himes's novels, has gained him his widest popularity in America. It deals with a Machiavellian Harlem
hostess, Mamie Mason, whose most towering ambition is
to win a place in society. She entices a variety of figures
from the white and Negro establishments to parties intended ostensibly to improve race relations. But Mamie
believes that race relations are best improved in bed, and
so the guests at her soirees generally manage to seduce
one another away from husbands, wives, lovers and so on
without any special regard to race.

The satire is presumably aimed at the pretensions of
certain elements of the Negro bourgeoisie and the race-
relations "moderates" who dominated the New York
scene a decade or so ago. The danger in writing novels
of this sort is that caricature implies a certain singleness
of purpose that makes the plot predictable. Himes must

therefore place his characters in more and more outra-
geous situations in order not to bore his readers. This
nearly succeeds, but the trouble is that too many of his
characters, black and white, male and female, are cut
from the same mold. They are all lesser Mamie Masons,
ambitious and unscrupulous and with only one thing,
more or less, on their minds. Hence the reader discovers
them jumbling in his thoughts, and he is forever turning
back pages in order to find out which one is who. Himes
ought really to have given each character a different dominant passion—and then thrown them all together in a
mad burlesque of manners and mores. As it is, however,
one sexual episode succeeds another, and although Himes
tries to brighten up his concoction with dashes of sadism,
masochism, and several other kinds of perversion, dimin-
ishing returns set in somewhere halfway through the
novel.

Pinktoes is not without its moments. Himes has a slap-
stick imagination and can write wildly funny scenes. He
can also do set pieces:

> Pinktoes is a term of indulgent affection applied to white
> women by Negro men, and sometimes conversely by
> Negro women to white men, but never adversely by ei-
> ther.

But there are too many of these definitionlike statements,
too many explanations: how Negroes are defined in
America, and why; how persons happen to be in such and
such a place when some unseemly event occurs; where
certain streets and houses are located in various parts of
New York; and so ad infinitum. Himes is constantly inter-
posing his own voice, sometimes condescending, up and
down the narrative line, like some roué schoolteacher in-
structing his prurient students. (The novel was originally
published in France, where such an account of the absurd
and funny ways Americans conduct their sex lives would
match a good many chauvinistic preconceptions.) In sum,
Pinktoes is a lightweight, aimed probably at capitalizing

on the success of *Candy* and like pornographic novels. If this was Himes's intent, he has succeeded. *Pinktoes* sells admirably.

Himes is a still-flourishing author in his early fifties. His long absence from America, however, is beginning to tell on his novels. Some of the details of his American setting are no longer quite accurate (in *Pinktoes* he places railroad tracks on West 10th Street in the Village.) And some of the attitudes he attributes to his white and Negro sophisticates are no longer fashionable (not publicly, at least), and in any event would no longer be generally articulated. Yet Himes has considerable narrative power and startlingly clear psychological insights. Perhaps what his novels now require is a European setting. It would be a shame if he were to allow his latest success to impair his progress as an artist.

Chapter VI

The Negro Church: James Baldwin and the Christian Vision

One of the few cultural institutions the Southern Negro transplanted to Northern soil with a modicum of success was his church. Initially its principal purpose was to serve the spiritual needs of the community, but as time went on the Church came to function as a kind of community newspaper linking the new migrants to their Southern past. In this respect the importance of the ghetto churches cannot be overestimated.

Migration to the cities constituted the most abrupt break in the Negro cultural experience since the days of the African slave trade. It was not simply the anxieties of the passage from a rural to an urban way of life—these, after all, were the afflictions of most Eastern and Central European immigrants around the turn of the century—it was more that the racial mores, prejudices, and barriers of the North were ill-defined, vague, and elusive so that the Negro felt he stood on ever-shifting grounds whose pitfalls were at once invisible and treacherous. Negro votes were courted in some parts of the country and discouraged in others. In New York, service trades such as barbering and catering, which at one time had been the almost exclusive province of Negroes, seemed suddenly to pass out of their hands and become the domain of Caucasian foreigners, while neighborhoods such as Greenwich Village, the Hell's Kitchen area, and the mid-Sixties of the West Side were suddenly theirs and almost as suddenly not, all in the passage of forty years or so after the Civil War. In the South, at least, a Negro knew where he stood, however barren and bitter his place. Above all, there existed in the South a pattern of interpersonal relationships among whites and Negroes—rooted, to be sure, in racial preconceptions, but for all that occasionally warm and recognizable—so closely interwoven had been the lives of both races over the centuries. But the white Northerner, when he was not downright hostile, treated Negroes with cold and faceless indifference. If he granted them greater self-expression, he seemed at the same time to be saying, "You may amuse me from time to time with your quaint and primitive antics, but in all significant areas of my life please keep away." For the Southern Negro migrant, the emotional stresses must have been intolerable.

It was precisely in this area that the Negro church functioned so effectively as an integrative force. It connected the Southern Negro with his former life, and gave him a socially acceptable outlet for his rage, his terror, and his frustrations—in its thinly veiled apocalyptic warnings, its evangelical fervor, and its promises of a better life to come. It also functioned as a political force, drawing together persons of diverse Southern origin and directing them toward goals which did not seem threatening to the established white power structure. Negro ministers were approached by white politicians who requested their support in elections, in return for favors to their communities and especially to themselves. This afforded the more successful Negro clergy—those with large congregations—some bargaining power. It never amounted to much, the way the world reckons these affairs, but it did provide a foothold of sorts in the great world beyond the ghetto.

The pluralistic and anarchic aspects of city life wrought their disintegrative forces on the Negro church just as they did on churches outside the Negro community. First- and second-generation urban Negroes tend, on the whole, to look less and less to evangelical Christianity as the source of their spiritual and emotional salvation. Still, the Messianic strain, the apocalyptic vision, the imagery and the fervor of the church, live on in the Negro community, fashioned now to more material and worldly ends. Indeed, the transfer of religious energies to political and social causes has swept along many Negro clergymen into what has since been called the Negro Revolt. The spirit of evangelism still permeates all areas of Negro culture.

Nowhere has this been so apparent as in the works of James Baldwin. In a sense, Baldwin is himself a symbol of this change. He was born in Harlem in 1924, the stepson of an evangelical minister, and was brought up in an atmosphere suffused with piety and puritanical rigor. His stepfather, stern, distant and authoritarian, insisted that his children devote as much spare time as they could to his views of Christian teachings. The evangelical church demanded much of the emotional and intellectual energies of its members, and it is a measure of Baldwin's commitment that he became a Young Minister at the age of fourteen. Baldwin's Christian ardor began to cool in favor of literature when he attended high school, but his writing career has been shaped by the rhetoric of evangelism and by his childhood understanding of the nature of the Christian's experience.

Underlying the American experience, there persists to

this day a strain of sheer Utopianism. Implicit in this vision is the notion of the goodness and purity of innocence as opposed to the evil of experience. The paradox lies of course in the fact that as Americans exercise themselves to recapture their innocence, they become more and more contaminated by their experience. This is one of the major themes of American letters. In a peculiar sort of way, Baldwin is at once the captive of this vision and, by virtue of his alienated status as a Negro, outside of it. Baldwin speaks everywhere of the "monstrous heart," the dark secrets of the soul—sinister and complex passions, the realities of which white Americans (as opposed to Europeans) refuse to recognize. As a Negro and a homosexual (hence doubly an outsider), against whom dreadful injustices have been perpetrated, he is particularly sensitive to this idea. And yet in his fiction, it is not the heart that destroys and betrays his protagonists, but what happens to innocence when the heart confronts the cruelly corrupt world. Thus Baldwin's characters generally end up more outraged and submerged than they began. But being true Americans, they continue to strive for what they know must ultimately defeat them.

This is not to suggest that the struggle against oppression and injustice is futile or undesirable, but rather that Baldwin does not recognize in himself the same failing of which he accuses white Americans: the inability to see that evil exists, that it is just as much an indelible portion of existence as is oxygen in the air. Were his characters to come to terms with their own hearts, they might be better able to survive. But this is asking for a level of maturity that few American authors have ever been able to achieve.

The only salvation Baldwin seems willing to offer in concrete or specific terms is the homosexual experience (in his latest novel, *Another Country*, 1962), but here Baldwin has retreated so far from the experiential world that the "truth" he has discovered is scarcely adequate. The homosexual theme is not unrelated to the kind of evangelical orientation Baldwin brings to his novels. What obscures the connection is Baldwin's own special relationship to his stepfather. In his essays, he writes that his stepfather was mean and distrustful and would not allow his children to get close to him. Baldwin's fiction, too, is replete with characters who are unable to establish relationships with their fathers, and who consequently reach out to other males for the kind of masculine love they were denied as children.

But even beyond the question of sexual development, there exists the problem of personal identity in a male-dominated society which only a father image can provide. The high proportion of fatherless Negro lower-class families has been noted many times by Negro authors and sociologists and psychologists generally. The sense of masculine identity is a very real problem for growing Negro boys. Add to this the emasculating effects of a white society that debases Negro men as clowns or "boys" and denies them the kind of meaningful work in which they could take pride.

The Negro church partially fulfills their psychic needs. By identifying themselves with a strong and wrathful Old Testament God, they assume vicariously the masculinity they have missed in their family and social lives. But in order for them to come to Him, they must abase themselves before Him, reject and condemn their worldly and sensual impulses and passively await the insemination of His divine spirit and grace. They thus become, momentarily at least, female in their quest for the masculinity that would provide them with identity. This becomes especially clear in the case of Baldwin, whose sexual and emotional development was stunted by an unloving father and an unresponsive society; evangelical Christianity provided him with some sort of psychic compensation.

Baldwin is, of course, aware of the latent sexual components of the religious experience. In one of his early short stories, "The Outing" (1951), he employs the setting of a church boat trip along the Hudson to describe an

adolescent's efforts to achieve the love and security of a
male companion after his father has publicly humiliated
him. Johnnie's pathos is reflected in the service that takes
place in the great hall of the boat, when the congregation
cries out passionately for the strength and guidance of
their God.

> Yet, in the copper sunlight Johnnie felt suddenly, not
> the presence of the Lord, but the presence of David; which
> seemed to reach out to him, hand reaching out to hand in
> the fury of flood-time, to drag him to the bottom of the
> water or to carry him safe to shore. From the corner of his
> eye he watched his friend, who held him with such power;
> and felt, for that moment, such a depth of love, such
> nameless and terrible joy and pain, that he might have
> fallen, in the face of that company, weeping at David's
> feet.

Baldwin's other stories do not use a specifically religious context, but the evangelical element is seldom very
far distant. Characters sing or hum snatches of hymns as
they go about their daily round of frustrations, and in at
least two of the stories, "Sonny's Blues" (1957) and
"Going to Meet the Man" (1965), a kind of ritual quality
lurks in the very essence of the narrative.

"Sonny's Blues" is the story of a jazz pianist who seeks
a means for expressing the grief and terror that rage
within his soul. The story is told by Sonny's brother, a
high-school teacher, who fears that Sonny may begin
anew an addiction to heroin from which, ostensibly, he
has just been cured. The climax of the story is reached
when Sonny happens upon some evangelists "testifying"
on a street corner. Later Sonny proceeds to a night club in
Greenwich Village where he hopes to renew his career as
a musician. After a few halting starts, he finds his expression with the band. In a sense Sonny "testifies"—and
the musicians and his audience are his witnesses.

> . . . I had the feeling that, in a way, everyone on the
> bandstand was waiting for him, both waiting for him and
> pushing him along. But as I began to watch Creole, I

realized that it was Creole who held them all back. He had
them on a short rein. Up there, keeping the beat with his
whole body, wailing on the fiddle, with his eyes half
closed, he was listening to everything, but he was listening
to Sonny. He was having a dialogue with Sonny. He
wanted Sonny to leave the shoreline and strike out for the
deep water. He was Sonny's witness that deep water and
drowning were not the same thing—he had been there,
and he knew.

. . . .

Freedom lurked around us and I understood, at last,
that he could help us to be free if we would listen, that he
would never be free until we did.

"Going to Meet the Man" is a unique story in the
Baldwin repertoire because here for the only time in his
fiction, he attempts to probe the mind of the violent op-
pressor. The story is related from the point of view of a
middle-aged sheriff who has been brutally engaging civil
rights demonstrators in a small Southern town. He tries to
understand their persistence, but their defiance and hatred
baffle him. After one especially grueling day, he attempts
unsuccessfully to make love to his wife; he is weary and
feels himself utterly depleted. His mind goes back to his
childhood when his father and mother took him to a
lynching at which seemingly the entire white community
was present. The whole scene is vivid in his memory—the
gouged and plucked eyes, the repeated dousing of gasoline
on the naked black body as he was periodically lowered
from a tree into the fire below, and finally the Negro's
castration by one of the executioners with a butcher knife.
The crowd—men and women alike—stares fascinated
and thrilled at the spectacle. The memory of this event
arouses in the sheriff a renewed desire for his wife. "Come
on, sugar," he whispers to his wife, "I'm going to do you
like a nigger, just like a nigger, come on, sugar, and love
me just like you'd love a nigger."

The weird and macabre ritual evidently serves to relieve the townspeople of their own sexual fantasies and

guilt. In punishing the Negro they have cleansed themselves, while at the same time they vicariously partake of his presumed potency. In effect Baldwin is saying that the white Southerner (and Northerner too for that matter) requires the Negro as a scapegoat for his sexual guilt and at the same time secretly desires him for his sexual power. It is interesting to note how Baldwin, even in this kind of extreme situation, discovers in his church-oriented psychology an understanding of his oppressors' behavior. Confession-expression, however enacted—symbolically in the lynching of the Negro, or among one's kindred spirits in a jazz club or a revival meeting—serves as a restorative of innate spiritual powers that have been depleted or atrophied by the experience of living in the mean void of the day-to-day world.

The prototypical church experience is related in Baldwin's first novel, *Go Tell It On The Mountain* (1953). Essentially it is the story of fourteen-year-old John Grimes's conversion, but the truly major figure of interest is John's father, Gabriel—and it is Gabriel, chiefly, around whom all the other characters' difficulties are centered. This is in a sense Baldwin's most ambitious book, in that he endeavors here not only to interconnect the lives and psychology of all the characters but also to relate these to the Southern Negro experience and the consequent shocks of urban slum living. The church, naturally, somewhat softens the impact—indeed makes their lives endurable, but it becomes clear in this novel that Baldwin regards the church as only a kind of temporary palliative and that dangerous trials lie ahead.

The novel is divided into three parts. The first part, "The Seventh Day," establishes the attitudes of John, his mother Elizabeth, and his Aunt Florence toward Gabriel —whom they alternately hate, fear, or distrust. Gabriel is a stern, aloof, self-righteous man with a scarcely concealed animosity toward John. He is a deacon of his church and commands his family in an imperious, hostile, arrogant manner. John is a sensitive, brooding boy, trou-

bled with a sense of sin, distressed at his worldly desires,
yearning guiltily to break free from the bounds of the
ghetto into the exotic white world beyond. After a particularly dreadful scene with his father in which the whole
family participates, he goes to the family church to perform some janitorial duties in preparation for the Saturday night "tarry" services. Here he meets Elisha, a
seventeen-year-old Young Minister. John feels a strange
physical attraction toward Elisha, and they tussle play-
fully. Later, several of the elders of the Church—the
Saints, as they call themselves—enter to sing and worship
and contemplate their souls. As the section closes, John's
mother, father, and aunt join them.

The tone of "The Seventh Day" is one of futility, of
unyielding frustration that permeates the lives of all the
characters, indeed of the Harlem community itself—and
the reader is made to feel that they and their posterity are
doomed to an existence of shabby poverty and soured
dreams. A significant passage details John's household
chores. His mother has asked him to clean the rug and
John thinks of Sisyphus pushing his boulder up the hill.

> He had John's entire sympathy, for the longest and
> hardest part of his Saturday mornings was his voyage with
> the broom across this endless rug; and, coming to the
> French doors that ended the livingroom and stopped the
> rug, he felt like an indescribably weary traveler who sees
> his home at last. Yet for each dustpan he so laboriously
> filled at the doorsill demons added to the rug twenty more;
> he saw in the expanse behind him the dust that he had
> raised settling again into the carpet; and he gritted his
> teeth, already on edge because of the dust that filled his
> mouth, and nearly wept to think that so much labor
> brought so little reward.

The narrowness of their lives compels each character to
seize his identity where he may, however senseless and
self-defeating it may appear. Thus Gabriel maintains an
authoritarian righteousness as head of his family even
though he knows that his lack of charity has alienated him

from their love. John cherishes his intelligence and his hatred of his father as being his own unique identity, and longs for the time he can emulate the white actress he had seen in a film that very day, who seemed to be telling the entire appalled and nasty world it could go to hell. But John knows in his heart that it is a fantasy, and that in some profound and mysterious way over which he has had no control, his fate has been long settled.

The stage has been thus set to examine the lives of Florence, Gabriel, and Elizabeth, in whom the seeds of John's fate are buried. In the second part of the novel, "The Prayers of the Saints," the three are seen at their prayers, each seeking the causes of his misery as he wanders back and forth over memories of the past.

It develops that Gabriel and Florence were brought up in the deep South by a pious mother whose other children had been taken from her during the bitter days of slavery. Despite their mother's constant prayers for their salvation, both Gabriel and Florence rejected her in her lifetime—Florence seeking a better life for herself in the North, while Gabriel stayed behind, sunk deep in sin, whisky, and disreputable women. Florence eventually married in the North, but her attempts to elevate her husband to bourgeois status failed utterly—and he left her for another woman, declaring that he wanted to remain the kind of common "nigger" she despised. Gabriel, meanwhile, experienced a religious conversion after his mother's death, and shortly thereafter became a preacher whose renown spread quickly throughout the region. He married a plain, sickly woman, Deborah, who bore him no children—a disappointment that bitterly rankled. At the height of his fame and despite himself, he had a brief liaison with a younger woman, Esther, whom he afterwards sent away when she told him she was going to have his baby. Esther died after the birth of their son, Royal, but Royal was brought up in Gabriel's town, and Gabriel silently watched him grow into a cocky and arrogant young man. Just prior to her own death, Deborah tells her

husband that Royal has been murdered in Chicago, and
that she has always suspected Gabriel of being his father.
Her dying words to Gabriel are that he had better repent.

Elizabeth met Florence when they both worked as
scrubwomen in a downtown New York office building.
Elizabeth, too, had suffered a severe, puritanical upbringing, under the guardianship of an unloving aunt in Mary-
land. When she was nineteen she came north to Harlem,
following a young man with whom she had fallen in love.
Richard, sensitive, tormented, and angrily bitter at the
white world, committed suicide, ignorant of the fact that
he had sired her baby. Florence introduced Elizabeth to
Gabriel after the latter had come North following the
death of his wife. Gabriel, evidently desiring to atone for
his neglect of Esther and Royal, regarded the unwed Elizabeth and her infant, John, as a kind of second chance
God had revealed to him. But Gabriel is incapable of
giving Elizabeth and John the kind of love and protection
they need. He is too full of his own sense of cosmic
importance, and lavishes all ardor on his own blood son,
Roy (Elizabeth has borne him three other children as
well), whom he regards as being part of God's strange
designs.

Florence, in turn, has hated Gabriel since childhood.
It was she who had been ambitious and desired an education to improve herself, but her mother unaccountably
devoted all her attention to Gabriel, whose worthlessness
and selfishness were patently obvious to all. It is interesting to note that Florence attempted to manage her husband in much the same way her mother had attempted to
manage Gabriel—and, like her mother, failed utterly.
Florence cannot understand where she was mistaken. She
has endeavored to emulate the middle-class life, but the
results are quite the same as if she had never tried. She is
old and alone now, living in abject poverty in a miserable
Harlem room. Her greatest residual passion is simply to
inflict pain on Gabriel, whom she blames for all her
wretchedness. She wants as well to protect Elizabeth,

whose marriage to Gabriel she feels partially responsible for.

It is clear, then, that the prayers of the Saints are not quite so spiritual as one might expect, but Baldwin, with nice irony, suggests that prayer is the only thing they have. And underlying their prayer is an immense anger, scarcely concealed, at a universe that has suppressed and choked them.

Part Three, "The Threshing Floor," is once more John's story. Falling prey unconsciously to a variety of emotions, John suddenly experiences a lengthy religious conversion, flinging himself prone on the floor of the church. It clearly festers in Gabriel that his bastard stepson—and not one of his own blood descendants—is now one of the elect. Florence, sensing her brother's bitterness toward John, threatens to reveal the contents of a letter that Deborah had sent her just before she died, which tells of Gabriel's dalliance with Esther and his subsequent neglect of his illegitimate son. Florence hopes, in so doing, to exact revenge on the brother she has hated all her life. John feels immense and mysterious forces at work in his life, and in an intensely passionate scene at the end of the service, he asks Elisha to remember him at these moments of his splendor regardless of what may happen to him in later years.

Each of the actors in Baldwin's drama has thus somehow "ritualized" the dominant passions of his life in the externals of religious worship. Gabriel remains embittered and righteous, Florence hating and wretched, Elizabeth bewildered and tormented, and it is suggested that John has now discovered and recognized his homosexuality. Religion has not liberated them from themselves permanently, but it has "objectified" their misery momentarily, and so has helped them to survive. This is especially true of John, whose fear and guilt and desire and despair and hatred have all been converted into a kind of meaningful delirium as he lies thrashing about the floor.

Ordinarily revelations of this nature produce an ability

to cope better with the tragic conditions of one's life; an enhanced self-awareness implies an enhanced possibility of human action to adjust to the conditions of existence. But unfortunately for Baldwin's characters, they are as utterly hopeless at the end of the novel as at the beginning. This is their private hell—and perhaps the Negro's; they know but they cannot act. From time to time their misery will be alleviated in the communal act of prayer but ultimately their despair is immovable. And one's final impression is of Baldwin's characters frozen in tableaux, arrested in prayer while a host of furies play about their heads and hearts.

In subsequent novels, Baldwin makes use of his church-oriented psychology in areas of subject matter one would not ordinarily expect. *Giovanni's Room* (1956) relates an American white youth's discovery of himself in the arms of his male lover, a tormented Italian bartender in Paris in the years shortly after World War II. David, who had been planning to marry, gives up his Giovanni when his fiancée comes to Paris. The engaged couple go to the south of France, where they live together for a while, but David cannot escape thoughts of Giovanni. His guilt is exacerbated by the knowledge that since he rejected him, the tender Giovanni has degenerated into a tramp among Paris pederasts, and has committed murder in a final act of desperation. David learns through the newspapers that Giovanni has been apprehended, tried, and found guilty, and is about to be executed. Shortly after Giovanni's death, David leaves Hella, his fiancée, whom he now finds physically revolting, and consorts for several days with homosexuals whom he picks up in bars on the Riviera. Hella finds him one night, and her new knowledge of her lover constrains her to break their engagement and return to America. The novel ends as David prepares to go back to Paris—doomed, he now knows, to suffer the endless rebuffs, humiliations, and torments of a homosexual.

The novel suffers on several scores, not the least of which is an absence of character growth or discernment.

Hella is portrayed as a bright but stereotypically shallow and neurotic American girl, devoid of the kind of passion and sensitivity David has found in Giovanni. Giovanni, on the other hand, is a wraithlike, childlike figure, who demands David's total love and attention. Aside from a few of the usual acid remarks about America and Americans that one has come to expect from sensitive foreigners in expatriate novels, Giovanni reveals scarcely any of the insight or depth of feeling that Baldwin attributes to him. The best that one can say here is that this is a recognition novel—David discovers that he is a homosexual (something that the reader could have told him on page three), and that he feels sorry for himself that he has discovered this dreadful knowledge. Even so, one suspects that David delights in his newborn sorrow and that in order to indulge it he has unconsciously manipulated the hapless Giovanni and the lonely, aggressive American girl.

The novel is not without its virtues. There is a certain economy—something suggestive of Poe, not only in narrative quality (the first person confessional of the dark and sinister ways of the heart), but in the overwhelming suggestion of horror that suffuses the atmosphere. If the ultimate horror proves itself not very horrible, Baldwin does manage some very good scenes that shriek with a kind of terror. Early in the novel he describes in macabre detail the homosexual bar in which David first meets Giovanni. Here the low life of the homosexual community congregates nightly—the male prostitutes and their aging wealthy patrons, the streetwalkers, the pimps, the near transvestites. Gathered together, gossiping, flirting, giggling in the unreal light of the bar, they suggest something of the demons in a Bosch painting. Baldwin's description of Giovanni's sordid and claustrophobic room—where David and Giovanni pass some of their most idyllic moments—is almost surrealistically rendered as the evil world which engulfs their innocence. But beyond the particular successes and failures of the novel are the ways in which Baldwin has transmogrified his Christian vision into the ostensibly revolutionary subject matter of his novel.

Christian love has here been transfigured into masculine love, the one redeeming grace in Baldwin's neo-Calvinist vision of a corrupt and depraved world. David's failure is that he has failed to "bear witness" to Giovanni's suffering—that he has failed to give him the love Giovanni demanded in order that he might survive. There follows then a curiously ambivalent attitude about the nature of human experience and of the human body. On the one hand, the world and experience become somehow the equivalent of the body, in that all three are viewed as the corruptive elements of the original purity of the soul. Giovanni and David cry out on more than one occasion about the vileness of their bodies and the world. Not surprisingly, this revulsion is directed more toward women than men, although Giovanni's homosexual bar appears as an inversion of paradise. Yet the female, Hella, is not inappropriately named either, in view of the pain David suffers when he is alone with her, in contrast to the heaven he knows with Giovanni.

On the other hand, the body and worldly experience, properly understood, are instruments of grace. This is something Giovanni knows by intuition, but which David has learned too late. The violation of innocence (or goodness), sad as this may be, is not totally evil, for it may lend depth to one's humanity. It is the religious paradox of good issuing from evil. But here innocence is discovered in the relationship of men who have not yet been contaminated with the notion of love as being exclusively heterosexual. For Baldwin it is only in homosexual love that innocence is experienced anew. The implication here is that innocence first existed in prepubescent youth. Giovanni, for all his worldly wisdom, is a child, a "baby," a "boy." David resents and simultaneously delights in mothering him. To David, the greatest pathos is in children whose innocence must one day be transgressed—by worldly experience—as was his.

> The city, Paris, which I loved so much was absolutely silent. . . . Behind the walls of the houses I passed, the French nation was clearing away the dishes, putting little Jean Pierre and Marie to bed. . . . Those walls, those shuttered windows held them in and protected them against the darkness and the long moan of this long night. Ten years hence, little Jean Pierre or Marie might find themselves out here beside the river and wonder, like me, how they had fallen out of the web of safety. What a long way, I thought, I've come—to be destroyed.

David's love affair with Giovanni exists outside chronological time—within the womb, as it were, at the beginning of creation.

> I remember that life in that room seemed to be occurring beneath the sea. Time flowed past indifferently above us; hours and days had no meaning. In the beginning, our life together held a joy and amazement which was newborn every day.

Baldwin depicts David's innocent beginning with Giovanni as an Old Testament Eden, the remembrance of which leaves him maddened with melancholy. He invokes further biblical imagery when he describes David's torment over whether or not to tell Giovanni he is leaving.

> . . . I moved toward him as though I were driven, putting my hands on his shoulders and forcing myself to look into his eyes. I smiled and I really felt at that moment that Judas and the Savior had met in me.

But if David's desertion of Giovanni is, in the last analysis, indefensible, it is also inevitable, because David is an American, whose civilization has taught him to deny the existence of pain and suffering and death. And it is precisely because he evades these realities that he is unable to accept the Eden Giovanni offers him, for Baldwin believes it is impossible for the adult to recapture his innocence until he accepts the tragedy of existence.

All of which leads Baldwin to describe another kind of innocence—one antithetical to Giovanni's—an American

innocence, carefully designed to ignore the terrors that
afflict the human heart by the simple refusal to admit their
possibilities. In effect this kind of innocence is evil, because it fails to allow the full potentialities of human life,
and thereby deprives persons of the full measure of their
sex and individuality, and it leads to the most brutal kinds
of racism, denying the humanity of others. Thus Baldwin
equates sexual and racial intolerance as deriving from the
same kind of mentality.

In *Another Country* (1962), Baldwin assumes an increasingly militant tone, focusing on the superiority of the
Negro and the homosexual by virtue of their extended
suffering. The homosexual and Negro are shown as one in
that they have both gleaned the value of suffering and are
thus both redeemable. The average white American, on
the other hand, because he has submerged a knowledge of
himself, dwells in a kind of psychic hell.

Indeed here Baldwin's America (mainly Greenwich
Village) is almost a literal hell in the oppressive heat of a
New York summer. The plot is much too complicated to
rehearse here in its entirety. There is no one central character, but the most sympathetic figure is a white homosexual actor named Eric, who returns from France and, in
the course of events, sleeps with an unhappily married
woman (Cass) and with the distressed white lover
(Vivaldo) of a Negro girl (Ida), thereby introducing
them to the mysteries of the human heart. Eric, however,
remains true in his fashion to Yves, a young Frenchman
with whom he had been living idyllically in France. At the
end of the novel Yves flies to America to rejoin Eric in
New York, the implication being that the two lovers reborn in their love will fashion a new heaven out of the
hell of America.

The most intriguing character in the novel is Rufus,
Ida's brother, whom Baldwin unfortunately kills off by
suicide early in the book. It is Rufus's ghost that haunts
all of the other major characters—indeed brings them
together. Rufus, a jazz musician, had fallen in love with a

white Southern girl, but the social and psychological pressures of living with Leona had so riven him that he killed himself. The people who knew and loved Rufus are made partly responsible for his death, although precisely where their responsibility lies is never quite made clear. Obviously they did not understand the extent of Rufus's suffering and hence were unable to bear witness—but, being white, they *could* not understand. And even if one were to grant the moral lassitude Baldwin attributes to them— and possibly some kind of a case might be made—the author lets them off much too easily. Vivaldo and Cass, for example, are awakened to a deeper understanding by sleeping with Eric. They are now presumably far more aware of the human condition—and especially the plight of the Negro. The homosexual experience is especially applicable to Vivaldo, who is undergoing a distressing relationship with his Negro mistress. Yet the reader is at pains to discover what magical properties Eric possesses. He is patient and forbearing and has yielded himself to countless lonely men who have clandestinely sought him out for the love they could find nowhere else, but he appears an amiable nondescript fellow. One wonders whether a heterosexual with the same generous qualities might not do the trick as well. But of course Baldwin's point is that a heterosexual is psychically ill-equipped to cope with loneliness, despair, and suffering—if he is white.

Rufus and Ida are in some respects the counterparts to Eric, for they live the dark and mysterious ways of the human spirit. Rufus dies because he has found no one to whom he could unburden his heart, but Ida, really an extension of her brother, is made of stronger stuff. Her most consuming passion is a rage at whites, because they are blind to the possibilities of their humanity, and because they use their power to curb the Negro life force. Since they are thwarted in so many other areas of self-expression, Baldwin can only display his Negro characters' superior prowess in jazz and sex. In these latter activities, Rufus and Ida are magnificent, and regard most whites with contempt. Ida tells Vivaldo:

> I used to see the way white men watched me, like dogs. And I thought about what I could do to them. How I hated them, the way they looked, and the things they'd say, all dressed up in their damn white skin and their clothes just so, and their little weak, white pricks jumping in their drawers. You could do any damn thing with them if you just led them along, because they wanted to do something dirty and they knew that you knew how. All black people knew that. Only, the polite ones didn't say dirty. They said real. I used to wonder what in the world they did in bed, white people I mean, between themselves, to get them so sick.

Like Eric, who has served so many lonely, desperate and unloved men, Ida, and Negro women like her, cater to the sick and impassioned needs of white men. Their sex serves to alleviate—at least temporarily—the anguish and the agony of the spiritual pariahs. They are, in a sense, priests, confessors, witnesses whose sexuality endows them with mysterious healing qualities, and because they are privy to the secret life of their supplicants, they possess a hidden knowledge and power that in some respects terrify the very persons who fly to them for succor. The terror is then translated into oppression and persecution in order to compel them to continue to play out their role as healers in the diseased sexual fantasies of white persons.

It is precisely this that most enrages and embitters Ida and Baldwin's other Negro characters. They must suffer and stifle and die in the miserable ghettos of America in order to appease the sickened psychic innocence of whites. It is at this juncture that Baldwin moves away from his vision of the Negro as the suffering servant, the scapegoat who returns his oppressors' scorn with love—to a view of the Negro fighting angrily, forcefully, vigorously for simple justice, for the assertion and sanctity of his humanity. It is here apparently that Baldwin (in this book, in any event) divides the roles of the Negro and the homosexual. Homosexuals like Eric, one feels, will persevere as figures of compassion upon whom the guilty and the stricken will unburden themselves. Negroes, however, must refuse to embody such a role in the future. The Negro and the homosexual thus assume two attributes of the godhead—the Negro representing justice, the homosexual, mercy.

But it must not be supposed that justice necessarily implies something harsh and vindictive. By asserting his claim to full humanity, the Negro may restore the white American to a truer, more childlike innocence. Ida shocks her white lover, Vivaldo, by reciting her affair with another white man. In effect she tells him frankly the bitter truths of being a Negro in a white world. Vivaldo, having just recently slept with Eric, is now prepared to accept reality on a much deeper level than he had previously allowed himself. He tells Ida he still loves her and they fall into one another's arms. Ida thus completes the process of stripping her lover of his American innocence.

> Suddenly, he reached out and pulled her to him, trembling, with tears starting up behind his eyes, burning and blinding, and covered her face with kisses, which seemed to freeze as they fell. She clung to him; with a sigh she buried her face in his chest. There was nothing erotic in it; they were like two weary children. And it was she who was comforting him. Her long fingers stroked his back, and he began, slowly, with a horrible, strangling sound, to weep, for she was stroking his innocence out of him.

Another Country possesses its own raw and violent power. And yet for all its heartfelt emotions, the novel scarcely gets anywhere. Somehow, sex and love and a vague knowledge of the enormities of the human heart are not sufficient to resolve the immense social, psychological, and moral issues of racism and alienation that Baldwin poses. They may represent a start but certainly not an end.

And even here Baldwin's anger somewhat shrouds his

art. His Negro characters all speak with the same voice
(Baldwin's), and sometimes the same syntax. Even his
white characters—with the exception of the formidable
Eric—although recognizable types, do not possess any
sharply defined individuality. For the most part they react
passively to the terrible emotions of their Negro friends—
and their motivations are pap.

In Baldwin's extended essay, *The Fire Next Time*
(1963), and his play, *Blues for Mr. Charlie* (1964), the
church militant advances at the expense of the church of
love and forbearance. *The Fire Next Time* is an extremely
moving piece. Baldwin begins by relating his early youth
in Harlem and all the attendant hardships, despair, and
frustration of the Negro community. He then describes
the particular appeal of the Black Muslim movement for
the Negro—Baldwin had had an audience with Elijah
Muhammad at his home in Chicago—despite the obvious
impossibilities of several of its specific doctrines. He concludes with some speculations regarding the future of the
Negro and the future of America itself. The essay is hardly
organized in any classic sense. Random thoughts enter
into the picture, and Baldwin frequently resorts to personal anecdotes to give substance to his own views. In
effect, the essay is a prolonged polemic against racism and
an almost wholesale attack on the entire American civilization of which racism is merely symptomatic. "Why,"
asks Baldwin, "should I want to be integrated into a burning house?"

The Negro must endeavor to extricate himself, but
Baldwin's sermon is something more than a declaration of
Negro independence; it is a clear statement that the white
man's salvation depends upon the Negro. Suppression of
the Negro is equated with suppression of knowledge of
the darkness from which men sprang and of the darkness
of death—hence, the terror of knowledge of life.

> One is responsible to life: it is the small beacon in that
> terrifying darkness from which we come and to which we
> shall return. One must negotiate this passage as nobly as

possible, for the sake of those who are coming after us. But white Americans do not believe in death, and this is why the darkness of my skin so intimidates them.

But the Negro who has survived in white America has always been aware of the precariousness of his life, and therefore knows its value and meaning.

> That man who is forced each day to snatch his manhood, his identity, out of the fire of human cruelty that rages to destroy it, knows, if he survives his effort, and even if he does not survive it, something about himself and human life that no school on earth—and indeed, no church—can teach.

The white man, if he is to become himself, must recognize the humanity of the Negro, and he must recognize that he has projected on the Negro his own fears and longings.

> The only way [the white man] can be released from the Negro's tyrannical power is to consent, in effect, to become black himself, to become a part of that suffering and dancing country that he now watches wistfully from the heights of his lonely power and, armed with spiritual traveler's checks, visits surreptitiously after dark.

To Baldwin, it is the height of absurdity and self delusion for the white man to assume the Negro wants to be his "equal." Indeed, quite the opposite: it is the white man who must strive to learn from the Negro.

> Why, for example—especially knowing the family as I do—I should *want* to marry your sister is a great mystery to me. But your sister and I have every right to marry if we wish to. . . . If she cannot raise me to her level, perhaps I can raise her to mine.

There is a considerable difference between Baldwin and previous generations of Negro polemicists who railed against the race-supremacy beliefs of white Americans. Baldwin assumes the superiority of Negroes (not genetically, but by virtue of their American experience, their

suffering) and pleads for the equality of *white* Americans.
And though here and there he prescribes love and mutual
understanding, the tone is largely one of outrage. Baldwin
warns that if his prescription goes unheeded, the holocaust
may be closer than most Americans care to imagine.

In *Blues for Mr. Charlie*, Baldwin translates his apocalypse into concrete social terms. The race war is not yet
quite upon us, but the play ends with preparation for a
Negro protest march in a small Southern town in which
its leader-minister keeps a gun in readiness concealed
under his Bible. The alternatives are clear: love or violence, the Negro can wait no longer. Baldwin's theater
resembles nothing so much—in form and fervor, at least
—as the protest dramas of the radical left in the thirties.
But the play is effective, for the emotions it arouses are
specifically vindictive and personally embarrassing to his
white audiences, which partly explains, no doubt, its failure on the Broadway stage. For Baldwin, the preacher,
not only thunders at his audience's failure of social and
human responsibility, but, far worse, he impugns their
sexuality and depicts them as more terrified of the possibilities of life than the Negroes they persecute.

If the bare outline of the plot appears somewhat hack-
neyed, this perhaps only proves that Baldwin can work
over old material with considerable skill. Related in flash-
backs and in swift scenes with the stage occasionally divided between backdrops of the Negro and white communities, the play deals with the murder of Richard, a young
man who has returned South after having flourished as a
musician on the Harlem stage. He is recovering from dope
addiction, and is thoroughly embittered at the life he met
in the North. In the course of events, Richard taunts and
insults the wife of Lyle, a white storekeeper, and when
Richard refuses to apologize, Lyle shoots him. There is a
trial, and of course the white jury exonerates Lyle. The
tense atmosphere is aggravated by the fact that the town's
Negroes have recently been demonstrating for their civil
rights. Parnell, a rich newspaper publisher, is divided in
loyalty between Lyle, a lifelong friend whose guilt he is

afraid to acknowledge, and Meridian, Richard's father, who leads the civil rights marchers. In addition, Parnell is secretly in love with Juanita, a Negro girl, who has always loved Richard. In the end, he opts to align himself with the Negroes, but though he is allowed to march in the same direction, they do not yet accept him as one of them.

Oddly, Baldwin has been accused of simplifying issues and persons, when in actuality he has done quite the opposite. Richard, who nurtures his being in hate, is presented as highly neurotic, obstreperous, and disagreeable, and perhaps unconsciously invites his own death. His heroism—if that is what it may be called—lies in his ability to articulate all the venom and bitterness he feels toward whites. It is an act of courage, but there is little else about him that is admirable. On the other hand, Lyle, the murderer, is portrayed compassionately, almost sympathetically. His entire identity requires that he believe himself superior to Negroes. This, moreover, is related to his heated animal attraction to Negro women as opposed to his warped and repressed sexual feelings toward his wife. Finally, there can be little doubt that Richard has taunted and challenged him almost beyond forbearance. Curiously, here and in the short story, "Going to Meet the Man," Baldwin draws his white Southern racists more believably than he does his white Northern liberals.

What presumably disturbed the critics, however—although none of them admitted it—was Baldwin's implication that whites generally, liberals and racists alike, are varying versions of Lyle. Parnell, for example, a decent and respectable fellow with whom liberals might identify, dreams of reaching out to the black nation just beyond his reach—and describes his own world as a dull gray envelope. Similarly, the other white characters are revealed in their day-to-day activities not as mean, but as devitalized. The Negroes, on the other hand, express depths of passion as they debate the courses of action they must take in their struggle.

The point, however, is not psychological but moral.

Given even the "worst kind" of Negro (Richard), and the most understandably provoked white man (Lyle), Baldwin is saying that simple justice demands the recognition of Negro humanity. The history that has produced Richard must never again be tolerated—even at the cost of violence. And it is fitting that Richard's father, a man of God, should say as the play ends, "You know, for us, it all began with the Bible and the gun. Maybe it will end with the Bible and the gun. . . . Like the pilgrims of old." Thus the steps from love to militancy are about to be taken, and a new history begins.

As an indictment of the sexual roots of racism, *Blues for Mr. Charlie* is sweeping. It is a propaganda piece with "real-life" characters—a rare achievement in protest drama. But the tentacles of the problem reach beyond society and sex into history, politics, and economics. Perhaps what is called for is surrealist-allegorical theater on the order of Genet's *The Blacks*. For racism—whatever else it is—is absurd, and it requires a more imaginative approach than Baldwin's Christian-Freudian interpretation.

What is encouraging is the new-found virility in Baldwin's prose. He recognizes the virtues of rage as well as its evils. And yet there are dangers as well. That Baldwin has the craftsman's way with words, there can be little doubt. As an essayist and polemicist he has few equals. But one wonders whether, as an artist, he may not now possibly consume himself in his recently recovered Jehovahlike rage.

Chapter VII

History as Blues: Ralph Ellison's
Invisible Man

In order to sustain himself in the American environment, the Negro has had to fashion a culture that could preserve some semblance of his dignity and at the same time would not appear to threaten the paranoid white civilization. Today most Americans are aware, if only sentimentally, of the work songs, spirituals, and legends that sprang from the ante-bellum South. But how many are aware that these form an integral portion of an underground culture of survival? One of the most characteristic expressions of Negro culture for the outside world, a carry-over from slavery days, is the grinning minstrel mask. The Negro has had to intuit the role the white man expected him to play, and

127

then to play it. But within the Negro community, an altogether different situation obtains. Movements, gestures, dress, speech rhythms, verbal imagery, all express nuances of meaning sealed off, in part at least, from the white world. Negro humor, Negro songs and dances, and Negro stories and fables all are passed on from elders to children as Negroes move about the length and breadth of the continent, seeking their place in the sun. And these are enriched by an insider's intimate knowledge of the white world—the kind of knowledge accessible only to domestics and nurses, mammies and menials, in whose presence such knowledge is considered "safe."

Ironically, despite the attempts of the white majority to isolate itself from Negroes, and despite the efforts of the Negro community to preserve its own ethnic identity and spiritual freedom, the Negro culture has permeated vast areas of the white population. As Leslie Fiedler has pointed out, white adolescents today sound and move and talk and dance more and more like their Negro counterparts. Perhaps they, too, seek a kind of expression that can assert their individuality in the face of a growing sense of isolation.

As has been indicated in earlier pages, it was not until the 1920's that Negro authors seriously attempted to deal with the folk materials in their culture. And when they did, the authors of the Harlem school treated Negro life self-consciously, as if somehow Negroness and poverty produced a superior kind of humanity, given to song and dance, and to a primitive, noble, exotic happiness as opposed to the corruption and neurosis of the surrounding white civilization.

The stark years of the thirties forced the Negro author to take a more realistic assessment of his situation. Frequently he labored under a structured ideology not altogether suited to his problems, but in any event he was required by this kind of discipline to relate what was unique in his culture to a broader over-all concept of history. During the first half of the decade the Communists appeared to champion an independent state located somewhere in the South, but after 1934 more and more stress was laid on full-fledged assimilation and integration into American life. This forced Negro intellectuals to examine even more closely their own ambivalent assimilationist and separatist views.

One of these was a young college student, Ralph Ellison, who came to New York in 1937 and began writing under the guidance and encouragement of a confirmed Party member, Richard Wright. Wright himself had written about the problem of Negro cultural identity and its place in a pluralistic society. Ellison almost immediately took up the dilemma, and in a sense devoted all his energies to its pursuit. After a long period of fits and starts in short stories, essays, and reviews, he achieved a major American novel, *Invisible Man* (1952).

No one could have been better suited, by virtue of his training and upbringing and experience, to undertake the challenge. Born in Oklahoma City in 1914, when caste lines were not yet so rigidly drawn as in other parts of the South, Ellison enjoyed a freedom to partake of the various crosscurrents of American life that were still sweeping across that near-frontier area. Not only did he encounter in his day-to-day experiences persons of different backgrounds, but he learned their songs, dances, and literature in the public schools. Moreover, he attended films and theater and read books avidly, and none of these suggested to him the "limitations" of Negro life. He dreamed the dreams of other American boys where the frontier spirit still obtained, and although he was aware of racism in the community, it never once occurred to him he was inferior because he was a Negro. "It was no more incongruous for young Negro Oklahomans to project themselves as Renaissance Men than for white Mississippians to see themselves as ancient Greeks or noblemen out of Sir Walter Scott."

He knew best, of course, his Negro culture, and he projected on his vision of the outside world the specificities of a Negro outlook. In his boyhood fantasies there existed Negro gamblers, scholars, cowboys, soldiers, movie stars, athletes, physicians, and figures from popular and classical literature. But jazz and especially blues provided him with the greatest sources of satisfaction. In his growing years, Kansas City jazz attained its ultimate refinement in the environs of Oklahoma City, and figures like Jimmie Rushing, Hot Lips Paige, Charlie Christian, and others became heroes to hosts of Negro boys. And if jazz was not regarded as being quite respectable in the schools he attended, he was given a rather impressive training in classical music so that he could make comparisons and perceive relationships. Thus for Ellison it was not simply a case of Negro culture standing apart, but a convergence in which Negro culture maintained its separate identity in a wider spectrum.

Not surprisingly, Ellison's understanding of his early life corresponds to his definition of Negro jazz. And ultimately it is jazz, and blues especially, that becomes the aesthetic mainspring of his writing. If literature serves as a ritualistic means of ordering experience, so does music, as Ellison well understands. And it is more to the rites of the jazz band than to the teachings of Kenneth Burke or the influences of Hemingway, Stein, Eliot, Malraux, or Conrad (persons whom Ellison mentions as literary ancestors and preceptors) that Ellison owes the structure and informing ideas of his novel. Particularly relevant is the attention Ellison casts on the jazz soloist. Within and against a frame of chordal progressions and rhythmic patterns, the soloist is free to explore a variety of ideas and emotions. But this freedom is not absolute. The chordal background of the other musicians demands a discipline that the soloist dare not breach. He is as much a part of the whole as he is an individual, and he may well lose himself in the whole before he recovers his individual identity. Finally, music, however tragic its message, is an affirmation of life, a celebration of the indomitable human spirit, in that it imposes order and form on the chaos of experience.

The delicate balance struck between strong individual personality and the group . . . was a marvel of social organization. I had learned too that the end of all this discipline and technical mastery was the desire to express an affirmative way of life through its musical tradition and that this tradition insisted that each artist achieve his creativity within its frame. He must learn the best of the past, and add to it his personal vision. Life could be harsh, loud and wrong if it wished, but they lived it fully, and when they expressed their attitude toward the world it was with a fluid style that reduced the chaos of living to form.

. . . .

For true jazz is an art of individual assertion within and against the group. Each true jazz moment . . . springs from a contest in which each artist challenges all the rest; each solo flight, or improvisation, represents (like the successive canvases of a painter) a definition of his identity: as individual, as member of the collectivity and as a link in the chain of tradition. Thus, because jazz finds its very life in an endless improvisation upon traditional materials, the jazzman must lose his identity even as he finds it. . . .

The hero of *Invisible Man,* in the course of a journey from the deep South to Harlem, assumes a variety of poses, most of which he believes in at the time, to fit the white man's definition of a Negro. But each of these roles fails him, and a kind of chaos ensues (barroom brawls, factory explosions, street fights, race riots and the like), for no one of them takes into account the fluidity and complexity of his individual being. At the end of the novel, hidden away in a forgotten basement room in an apartment building, the hero comes to no true resolution of his dilemma except the realization that his humanity is invisible to most persons, Negroes as well as white, and that he must discover for himself what he thinks, feels, and is. Yet the mere act of telling his story in novel form has given order to the meaninglessness of his experiences, and has thus become an affirmation, a celebration of life. He intends, he says, to ascend to the surface soon, to have another "go" at the world.

The novel is no more than a recapitulation of the pain

the hero has suffered in his twenty or so years—the telling
of which is its own catharsis. No social message, no system of beliefs, no intellectual conclusions arise from his
tale other than his own consolation in telling it. Yet in the
telling, he cannot but see the comically absurd aspects of
his existence, of all Existence—and his narration is therefore not without humor. (Ellison told one interviewer that
he thought he had written a very funny book.) *Invisible Man* is tragic in the sense that it celebrates the hero's
capacity to endure, comic in the sense that he avers the
fecundity of life, the wealth of the possibilities he may
choose (and he often chooses wrongly) amidst the abun-
dance of chaos.

Ellison has several times described this view of life as
blues. In 1946 he wrote:

> The blues is an impulse to keep the painful details and
> episodes of a brutal experience alive in one's aching con-
> sciousness, to finger its jagged grain, and to transcend it,
> not by the consolation of philosophy but by squeezing
> from it a near-tragic, near-comic lyricism. As a form, the
> blues is an autobiographical chronicle of personal catas-
> trophe. . . .

Ellison also sees the blues as serving a ritual function.

> The blues speak to us simultaneously of the tragic and
> comic aspects of the human condition and they express a
> profound sense of life shared by many Negroes precisely
> because their lives have combined these modes. . . . This is
> a group experience . . . and any effective study of the blues
> would treat them first as poetry and ritual.

Invisible Man opens with a prologue in which the
hero, in his secret basement room, announces he is about
to recite the catastrophic events of his life. He has rigged
up along the walls 1,369 electric lights whose power he
has illegally sequestered from the Monopolated Light and
Power Company in order to shed light on his invisibility.
He has been playing a Louis Armstrong record, the refrain of which runs: "What did I do/To be so black/And

blue?" In a sense, this refrain implicitly follows each of the major episodes of the novel. As his attempts to play out the roles that whites have assigned him (each of them different, but all of them dehumanizing, like variations on a theme) meet with disaster, the hero in effect asks himself Armstrong's punning question. He has tried to play the game according to the rules but has each time discovered himself more bruised. Thus each episode serves almost as an extended blues verse, and the narrator becomes the singer. The epilogue brings us back to the present; the reader is returned to the basement room, and the hero tells us that despite his psychic wounds (he has dreamt that he has been castrated), he has not yet given up on life. Hence the novel ends as it had begun, just as the last verse of a blues is frequently the same as the first.

Since the blues, according to Ellison, is by its very nature a record of past wrongs, pains, and defeats, it serves to define the singer as one who has suffered, and in so doing it has provided him with a history. As the novel develops, the hero takes on the role of a Negro Everyman, whose adventures and cries of woe and laughter become the history of a people. As a high-school boy in the South, he is a "Tom"—little better than a darky entertainer; in college, a Booker T. Washington accommodationist. When he moves North, he works as a nonunion laborer and then flirts for a while with Communism. Finally, he becomes a Rinehart, Ellison's word for the unattached, alienated, urban Negro who deliberately endeavors to manipulate the fantasies of whites and Negroes to his own advantage. But besides being a kind of symbolic recapitulation of Negro history, the blues structure of the novel suggests a philosophy of history as well—something outside racial determinism, progress, or various ideologies, something indefinably human, unexpected and perhaps nonrational.

In one sense the Negro since Emancipation has telescoped the American experience, passing from an agrar-

ian existence to a highly industrialized urban life. In another sense this history is enigmatic—not only invisible
but unformed—a history in which chance and accident
act as principles in a designless universe. So long as men
demand predetermined patterns of their universe, in order
to reassure themselves that existence is not chaotic
(which it is), they will demand that Negroes play out
certain roles to conform to these patterns. But there is an
issue of "necessity" involved. The Negro, like any other
man, is unresolved nature, mysterious and complex, and
cannot by the very exuberance of his being long play out
these roles. When this occurs, illusion is then momentarily stripped away and chaos is seen for what it is. But
the white man, terrified at these realities, proceeds to
force upon the Negro still another role to suit yet another
fancied pattern of existence. Does this mean that history
and life need be perceived as unmitigated purposeless-
ness? In effect Ellison never truly resolves the question
aesthetically. But he seems to be saying that if men recognize first that existence is purposeless, they may then be
able to perceive the possibility of shaping their existence
in some kind of viable form—in much the same manner
as the blues artist gives form to his senseless pain and
suffering.

As a beginning, let us look at the Prologue. The hero,
as he sits in his basement room listening to his Louis
Armstrong record, passes in illusion into his slave past. In
his dream an old slave woman tells him she has poisoned
her beloved white master because he reneged on his
promise to free her. Her master had sired her two sons
who have always hated him. Thus is established the love-
hate relationships of whites and Negroes.

As the novel proper opens, the hero recalls his grandfather's dying words: "I never told you, but our life is a
war and I have been a traitor all my born days, a spy in
the enemy's country ever since I give up my gun in the
Reconstruction." He goes on to advise, "I want you to
overcome 'em with yeses, undermine 'em with grins, agree

'em to death and destruction, let 'em swoller you till they vomit or bust wide open." These then will be the tactics the Negro will employ for survival in years to come. He will pretend to agree to his invisibility until reality strikes down the white man for his obdurate blindness. The novel then proceeds to record the hero's various initiation rites into invisibility wherein the white man accords him several identities—none of them human. Ultimately his is a journey into self-recognition. He recognizes first that he is invisible—and second, that he is a man.

The hero follows his grandfather's advice, though at first he understands it only dimly. He is vaguely disturbed, of course, that in acting out the white man's fantasies he is expressing his own antagonisms, but his real enlightenment does not come until later. The tone of the first half of the novel is that of an almost Gulliverlike innocence. He relates objectively how "sincerely" he attempts to fulfill his roles, how deeply he believes in them. As a high-school graduate, he is invited to deliver his valedictorian address on humility as being the "very essence of progress" to a smoker of the leading white citizens of the town. But before he is allowed to do so, he must first, along with other Negro boys, observe the gyrations of a nude blond belly dancer, and then fight these same boys half-naked and blindfolded on an electrified rug for what they presume to be gold coins that have been thrown their way. The ritual, of course, serves to gratify the prurience of the white spectators since they can vicariously partake of the Negro's virility which they can humiliate at the same time. The Negro meanwhile learns that in order to acquire even a particle of material wealth, he must first debase himself before the white man. The hero is finally allowed to give his speech (at first scarcely anyone appears to be listening), but there is very nearly an explosive situation when, by a slip of the tongue, he mentions social equality. At the end of his speech, he is given a briefcase in which, during the course of his subsequent adventures, he will place tokens and mementos of the various identities the Negro has assumed during his history.

The second major episode takes place in a Southern Negro college whose buildings and environs—magnolias, honeysuckle, moonlight—the hero describes in glowing (faintly satirical) terms. The college has been endowed in large part by Northern liberals who, since Reconstruction, have endorsed Booker T. Washington's twin principles of equality and caste submission—not only a logical contradiction, but, again, a kind of blindness to reality. But here Ellison is suggesting as well that the Northern white liberal philanthropist demands the invisibility of the Negro no less than his Southern racist counterpart, in order to conceal from himself his ancestors' complicity in Negro slavery. Ellison, in this portion of the novel, employs, in addition, constant allusion to Negro history as a means of discovering the Negro's present invisibility. The hero relates, for example, the presence on the campus of a statue of the Founder, a former slave, who is removing (or placing?) a veil from (or on?) the eyes of a kneeling Negro. Was Negro enlightenment simply another guise of keeping the Negro in the dark, invisible from himself?

There are mellow scenes of students assembled in chapel singing symphonic and devitalized slave spirituals for white patrons. Or a moving and eloquent address by an ancient Negro minister rehearsing the life, trials, and achievement of the Founder. The Founder's immense sacrifices, the students are told (probably for the thousandth time) in wonderful old-fashioned ringing rhetoric, have made possible the progress and happiness they enjoy today. At the close of his speech, the minister stumbles as he leaves the rostrum and the students suddenly realize that the minister is himself blind.

Some of the best passages in the novel occur when the hero, an honors student, acting as chauffeur to one of the white patrons who has been visiting the college, inadvertently drives him beyond the picturesque manicured environs of the college campus past the old slave quarters.

This is a part of the countryside Mr. Norton has never before seen and he is met with reality for the first time. The habitations are unchanged since ante-bellum days and the Negro peasants living thereabouts are regarded as little better than barbarians by the middle-class college community. Norton talks to one of them, Jim Trueblood, who recounts the fantastic events relating to his incest with his daughter, which has made him a celebrated figure among the whites in the county. (Respectable Negroes are ashamed.) Norton, who had earlier told the hero of his idealized attachment to his deceased daughter, listens to Trueblood's story stricken and entranced. At one point he exclaims, "You have looked at chaos and are not destroyed!" Trueblood has acted out Norton's own unconscious longings for his daughter. He has thus served the same psychological purposes for Norton (and other whites) as the half-naked struggling boys at the smoker. At the close of Trueblood's story, Norton apparently suffers a heart attack, and the hero takes him to a Negro roadhouse, the Golden Day, in order to revive him with whisky. As luck would have it, they arrive at about the same time as a group of Negro mental patients, shell-shocked veterans of World War I, who pay periodic visits under guard for a respite of drinks and disreputable women. A wild riot erupts and Norton is hurt and hustled out, but not before one of the veterans tells him that for all his vaunted philanthropy, the Negro is not a human being but a "thing," a cipher to satisfy his guilt and his cravings for adulation and love.

Here Ellison suggests the results of a hundred years of white liberal patrimony of the Negro. Large financial donations may afford the givers some illusion of having fulfilled their moral obligations, but failure to recognize the Negro's humanity has produced only a worsening of pain. Earlier in the novel, Norton had told the hero that the Negro is his destiny. "*You* are important because if you fail, I have failed. . . . I am dependent upon you to learn my fate. Through you and your fellow students I become, let us say, three hundred teachers, seven hundred trained mechanics, eight hundred skilled farmers, and so on. That way I can observe in living personalities to what extent my money, my time and my hopes have been fruitfully invested." Although Norton would like to believe the college is a monument to his efforts, in reality the maddened rioting veterans of the Golden Day are his true fate. They represent the logical absurdity of his dream, for they are not, like Trueblood, Negro peasants bound to the soil, but testimonials to Negro progress—doctors, lawyers, teachers. Thus has Ellison married elements of the Negro's invisible past to the Negro's invisible present: slavery (Trueblood), Reconstruction (the college campus), philanthropy (Norton), and World War I (the veterans)—all resulting in a chaos called The Golden Day.

When Norton is finally returned to the campus, the president of the college, Dr. Bledsoe, a self-effacing, ingratiating figure (especially in the presence of whites), is infuriated at the hero for exposing their white friend to the seamier side of Negro life. He threatens the hero with expulsion and when the latter protests that he had only been attempting to carry out Norton's request for whisky, the president explodes that one does not obey the white man, one only *seems* to. In effect, Bledsoe is the living illustration of the hero's grandfather's dying words. He has "overcome 'em with yeses." He informs the hero that he would not have achieved his exalted position had he not played along with the white man's Negro fantasies and cleverly manipulated these psychoses to acquire power for himself. He has the facility, he says, of making the white man do his bidding by insinuating his ideas into the white man's fantasies. Thus Bledsoe, despite his abject and humble exterior, is one of the most powerful men in the South, who sustains a vested interest in keeping the Negro invisible.

Ellison moves from the white-Negro Southern power structure to the Negro's Northern plight. Bledsoe has ostensibly suspended the hero for the summer months but has provided him with letters of identity to important New York capitalists who might employ him. The journey North has a blues ring, especially when the hero discovers that Bledsoe too has deluded him with false promises. But the hero does manage to find work at the Liberty Paint Company, whose motto reads, "Keep America Pure with Liberty Paints." His first task is to infuse ten drops of a blackish substance into buckets of a white base liquid and stir, the result being a product called Optic White which is used in repainting national monuments. Here Ellison's allegory becomes a little too obvious.

The hero is next assigned to work at the furnaces of a basement, three levels underground, with a strange little Negro foreman named Lucius Brockaway. It develops that Brockaway, who has charge of all the immensely complicated machinery below ground—boilers, furnaces, cables, pipes, wires, and so on—is indispensable in running the plant. Efforts to displace him with white engineers have resulted in a total breakdown of production. Moreover, he has worked for Liberty Paints since its inception. "Everybody knows I been here ever since there's been a here—even helped to dig the first foundation." Later he tells the hero that they "are the machines inside the machine." From simple allegory Ellison has moved to a more subtle kind of symbolism. Somewhere beyond the narrative level, he is saying that America has depended from the start on the unacknowledged skills and sacrifices of Negro labor.

But if Brockaway is the indispensable man, he is also the white capitalist's man as well. He is fiercely opposed to labor unions, and when he learns that the hero, during his lunch hour, inadvertently stumbled onto a union meeting (in which, incidentally, a discussion had been proceeding regarding the employment of nonunion Negro workers), he accuses the hero of treachery and betrayal. He attacks the hero and the two wrestle weirdly in the underground chamber—a Northern echo of the battle of the boys at the white citizens' smoker. Just when the hero believes that Brockaway has finally reconciled himself to his presence, a boiler explodes and the hero awakens to discover himself in the plant hospital.

The hero's Northern industrial experience has thus far found him caught somewhere between a hostile labor movement, a suspicious Negro working class (Brockaway), and an employer who evidently uses him to undermine the union. His situation is further aggravated by the Depression, which inevitably strikes hardest at Negroes. The hero is released from the hospital and dismissed from his job ("You just aren't prepared to work under our industrial conditions"), after an operation intended to produce in him a new and more docile personality. During the operation—he is placed in a glass-covered box and connected with electrodes—he hears one skeptical doctor say, "It would be more scientific to define the case. It has been developing some three hundred years—" Yet the operation does not altogether remove his identity. He remembers snatches of folklore and songs his grandmother had sung to him as a child which seem strangely applicable to his situation. The past lives on, then, in the present, and whatever else urban life and the Depression may have done to him, they have given him a greater sense of pride and an awareness of his history.

The hero now strides through the streets of Harlem somehow reassured by the swarming black life about him. He eschews the black middle class that hopelessly and ludicrously models itself on the white bourgeoisie—his first place of residence, Men's House, is a haven for such persons—and lives in a boardinghouse run by Aunt Mary, a formidable mother-earth figure who cares warmly for the lost and bewildered children of her native Southland. Nor is the hero any longer ashamed of Southern Negro foods that identify him with a slave and peasant ancestry. On one occasion he stops to purchase a yam from a Southern street vender. "I am what I am," he says as he bites into the hot buttered delicacy.

But if urban life awakens the hero to emotions of a

specific Negro historical identity, as opposed to what Ellison once described as Southern rural "pre-individualistic attitudes" (that is, an almost total absence of selfhood, a passive attitude toward oneself as being part of an amorphous black mass), the Depression expands these feelings to include an active sense of social responsibility the hero now shares with many other city Negroes. And the latter part of the novel deals with some of the forces that endeavored to make political use of the new awakening in Negro communities.

Black nationalism, the first of these, is represented in the figure of Ras the Exhorter, an exotic West Indian extremist. The hero sees Ras violently addressing a street corner gathering when he first arrives in Harlem from the South. He pays little attention at the time but when he later involves himself with the Brotherhood (the Communist Party), Ras and his followers play a distinct role in his experiences. Ras, who suggests something of the colorful Marcus Garvey, preaches a doctrine of complete black virtue coupled with an utter distrust of the white man. Attired in Ethiopian garb, Ras makes a ludicrous figure, but his eloquence and passion more than make up for his lack of "program." As one of the hero's companions later puts it, Ras works on the "inside"; that is, he articulates the frustration, suspicion and anger the Negro has suppressed about his American experience.

The hero is recruited by the Brotherhood when, after witnessing the physical eviction of an elderly Negro couple from their tenement, he delivers a fiery speech protesting the injustice of it all to a gathering street crowd. Even here, Ellison suggests the specific Negro history that has ultimately placed the unhappy pair on the dreary Harlem sidewalk. He cites the pathetic paucity of personal effects they are allowed to keep, among them a small Ethiopian flag, a tintype of Abraham Lincoln, a manumission paper dated 1859, a pair of "knocking bones" used in minstrel shows, some faded and void insurance policies, and a "yellowing newspaper portrait of a huge black man with the caption: 'MARCUS GARVEY DEPORTED.' " The hero's passionate outburst evokes a small riot, whereupon the white evicters are pummeled and the Negro couple are triumphantly returned to their flat. The hero manages to escape before the police arrive, but his performance has meanwhile attracted the attention of one of the Brotherhood members, who pursues him and asks him to join the organization. His function, it appears, will be to address Negro gatherings on behalf of Brotherhood principles. He would, of course, have to learn what these are—and, after some reluctance, the hero agrees to do so.

Ellison perhaps devotes too much space proportionally to the Communist wooing of the Negro, but these are experiences he knew, after all, firsthand, and the Marxist emphasis on Negro history as being part of a larger dialectical process must have appealed to Ellison's ingrained aesthetic sense. In any event, his hero's Communist experiences are too complicated to chronicle fully. He becomes an authentic Harlem "spokesman," but even when he is most blinded by his Marxist rhetoric, there persist in the marrow of his being some suspicions regarding the relevance of his Negro experience to the notions of history he publicly upholds. Indeed, Ras's violent and chauvinistic opposition to Brotherhood ideals is closer to what the hero knows to be true. What he finally learns in the course of his radical adventures is that even for the Brothers, the Negro is a thing, an object, an instrument of power politics and of preordained historical design, rather than a divinely complex and complicated human mystery. He concludes, therefore, that he has been as invisible to the Brotherhood as he has been to all the others, and that the Brothers require his invisibility in order to delude themselves concerning their own historical identity. The white Brotherhood chieftain, Brother Jack, wears a glass eye, implying, of course, that he perceives only mechanistic history ("necessity") and not the accidental nature of human beings.

Yet his experiences as a radical are not a total loss. For

one thing, the hero, like his author, has acquired an education of sorts regarding the Negro's role in history. If what the hero learns is at considerable variance from what the Brotherhood wanted him to learn, he does nonetheless take away with himself an added sense of his own importance. Second, and possibly more important, is that in making him a Harlem leader, the Brotherhood has unwittingly given him access to his fellow Negroes on a level he had hitherto seldom achieved. He discovers to his astonishment (and to the chagrin of the Brothers) a bond of love and shared experience that the outside world can never know.

In one of his first performances for the Brothers, he addresses an assembly of Negroes on the question of rent evictions. His speech is full of platitudes regarding the prior blindness of Negroes to omnipresent exploitation and new perceptions of the future in the light of Brotherhood principles—when suddenly he finds himself saying words he had not planned:

> I feel that here, after a long and desperate and uncommonly blind journey, I have come home. . . . Home! With your eyes upon me I feel that I've found a true family! My true people! My true country!

As a result of his speech, his reputation is established. He begins to campaign against rent dispossessions, but then quite unexpectedly he is transferred downtown, ostensibly for further indoctrination. Upon his return several months later, he learns that the agitation he had begun so successfully has lost nearly all its momentum and that the community has become hostile to the Brotherhood for its betrayal. When he attempts to pick up the pieces, he is disturbed to find his efforts are met with resistance within the Brotherhood. His anxieties are further aroused when he learns that Tod Clifton, his closest Harlem comrade and a Brotherhood lieutenant, has vanished. Quite inadvertently, the hero one day stumbles upon Tod on a mid-town street, illegally hawking dancing, flouncing, string-operated paper Sambo dolls before a crowd of amused onlookers. The hero is disgusted, but Tod, in effect, is "signifying" by his actions that he has been as much a Sambo puppet working for the Brotherhood as he is now, vending paper dolls that advertise his humiliation. Later the hero witnesses Clifton being shot to death by a policeman who had been trying to arrest him.

On his return subway trip to Harlem, the hero ponders Clifton's death, and then as he observes a trio of zoot-suited adolescent Negro boys sitting quietly in front of him, he realizes that:

> They were men out of time—unless they found Brotherhood. Men out of time, who would soon be gone and forgotten. . . . But who knew (and now I began to tremble so violently I had to lean against a refuse can)—who knew but they were the saviors, the true leaders, the bearers of something precious? The stewards of something uncomfortable, burdensome, which they hated because, living outside the realm of history, there was no one to applaud their value and they themselves failed to understand it. What if Brother Jack were wrong? What if history was a gambler, instead of a force in a laboratory experiment, and the boys his ace in the hole? What if history was not a reasonable citizen, but a madman full of paranoid guile and these boys his agents, his big surprise! His own revenge? For they were outside, in the dark with Sambo, the dancing paper doll; taking it on the lambo with my fallen brother, Tod Clifton (Tod, Tod) running and dodging the forces of history instead of making a dominating stand.

Here then is the blues theme as applied to history. The accidental, the unplanned, the unforeseen variables of history are symbolized by the presence of the Negro, who because of his invisibility should not logically exist, but who nonetheless endures and may, on some future occasion, transform events overnight. And the mere fact of his survival, despite sufferings, defeats and repressions, represents an affirmation of life that undercuts any "system" of history. Because human beings are involved, history, like blues, records only the possibilities of existence.

The hero organizes a huge procession for the dead Clifton on the streets of Harlem (in the absence of explicit instructions from the Brotherhood hierarchy) and delivers an oration. ("His name was Clifton, Tod Clifton, he was unarmed and his death was as senseless as his life was futile.") The Brotherhood at once makes plain its opposition to the hero's militancy and he is now finally convinced he has once more been betrayed. He intends as vengeance to delude them as they had all along been deluding him. He will follow his grandfather's advice: "overcome 'em with yeses, undermine 'em with grins" until the entire Harlem community erupts in their faces. He will pretend to them that their more pacific plans to organize the community are eminently successful, while in reality he knows that Harlem seethes with social and racial tensions, not the least of which are aimed at the Brotherhood.

Since much of the hostility of the community is directed toward him as being an instrument of a white man's organization, the hero determines to take a new identity. He settles for a wide-brimmed white hat and dark glasses—but the disguise works only too well. He is constantly being stopped on the street by persons who mistake him for someone named Rinehart. But on each occasion they know Rinehart as possessing a different occupation. For some, he is evidently a numbers runner, for others a gambler or a lover, or a minister of an occult church, a "spiritual technologist," a seer of the "Unseen." The hero is thus reborn as Rinehart, whose "world was possibility . . . [a] vast seething hot world of fluidity" in which Rinehart plays many roles. For the real Rinehart had evidently perceived the Negro's world as an undesigned Chaos in which he could have as many images as he wished. Is this not the white man's world as well, the hero wonders, since no understanding of history can have any validity if it fails to recognize the Negro's existence?

Here Ellison and his hero stand at the brink of existential
despair, where values such as love, honor, and integrity
have no meaning.

But before he can resolve his disturbed vision, the hero
is pulled back into a Harlem uprising of destruction and
violence for which he is in part responsible. Mobs roam
the streets, stores are plundered, buildings burn, and Negroes and police shoot at one another at street crossings
and from behind barricades of wreckage. Ras rides about
on a horse, spear in hand, exhorting his followers to drive
the white man out of Harlem. And the hero glides in and
out of scenes of destruction like a master of chaos. On one
occasion he sees a group of men plan and execute the
arson of a wretched tenement house. First they ascertain
that the building is cleared of all tenants; then they start a
conflagration on each of the floors. The entire operation is
very methodically carried out. What astounds and delights
the hero is that here is something that Negroes have done
by themselves—not under the directions or command of
"the man."

> They've done it, I thought. They organized it and car-
> ried it through alone; the decision their own and their own
> action. Capable of their own action. . . .

The hero does not, however, stay long with the arsonists;
eventually he discovers himself being pursued down the
streets by Ras's men, who want to kill him. (The Rinehart glasses are shattered, and he finds himself once more
a vulnerable identity.) Having eluded his pursuers, he is
chased again, this time by a pair of white hoodlums who
have evidently come to Harlem in search of loot. He dives
into an open manhole and ultimately finds his way into
the discarded basement room which will become his
home.

In the basement room the hero decides that he has all
along been invisible. But before he can determine who he
is, Ellison makes him discard the contents of the briefcase
he has been carrying ever since the night of the smoker.
In the course of his life he has collected a number of

objects which he has "unthinkingly" stuffed in his briefcase. In effect these represent not only his past identities
but the roles the Negro has played in history. At one
time or another, the briefcase has contained a small an-
tique cast-iron bank for coins molded in the figure of a
red-lipped, minstrel Negro (economic exploitation), a leg
shackle (peonage), his high-school diploma (his Jim
Crow education), Clifton's Sambo doll (his minstrel
role), a letter from Jack identifying him as a Brother, and
his dark Rinehart glasses. In jettisoning these, as it were,
the hero can come to a true recognition of himself.

In isolating the historical theme of Ellison's blues, one
does not, of course, begin to do justice to the novel. The
narrative pace is swift and engaging, and the hero's adventures possess their own intrinsic interest. Moreover,
Ellison's symbols seldom intrude as they explain, and yet
are quite as original as they are functional. Nonetheless,
splendid and ambitious as Ellison's novel is, it does not
quite succeed. Perhaps one reason is that his hero, owning
no identity or at best an invisible one, does not create in
the reader any real empathy. He is not a lovable rogue,
nor a goodhearted innocent, but merely a passive figure
who, for the most part quite mindlessly, allows things to
happen to him. This was of course Ellison's intention, but
given the sustained length of the novel and the colorless-
ness of the protagonist, the reader is made more and more
aware that he is reading a book. There is simply too much
distance between the reader and the hero and one finds
oneself subconsciously congratulating the author for the
deftness with which he moves his character along, rather
than paying attention to his troubles or his meaning. Secondly, there is a singleness of theme—the hero's invisibility—and episode after episode plays variations on this
theme. It is as if one were compelled to listen to a marve-
lous blues extended to symphonic length. One may ad-
mire its various parts, but wish after a while for a different kind of movement—to catch oneself up in surprise or
elation or another level of comprehension.

In all fairness, Ellison attempts to do this. The tone of

the hero changes from that of a gullible innocent in the beginning to that of a straightforward narrator somewhere midway in the novel, to that of a somewhat more sophisticated observer of himself later on. And Ellison himself has said of his novel that it moves stylistically from naturalism to expressionism to surrealism—all of which is true. But these are, after all, effects, and the single idea still dominates. One somehow expects more, for all its richness, and the "more" is seldom forthcoming.

Which brings us once again to the thematic weakness of the novel. For Ellison's hero simply has nowhere to go once he tells us he is invisible. He does indeed, in the Epilogue, say that he intends to rise again and try his hand at life, that he has faith in democratic principles, and that life itself is its own excuse despite the blows it has dealt him. But there is no evidence in the text to fortify his beliefs. The blues singer has depths of feeling to begin with, but Ellison's hero has just begun to learn to feel as the novel ends.

One dwells on these issues because *Invisible Man* is so very nearly a great book. Perhaps Ellison himself, caught somewhere between Negro blues and the symphonic complexities of Western experience, has yet to find his footing. Or possibly his position as an American Negro, an invisible man, will make it impossible for him to find his way. One wonders. His second novel, now fifteen years in the writing, is yet to be published. When it appears, perhaps we shall have the answer.

Chapter VIII

The New Nationalism: Malcolm X

No Negro leader has so captured the imagination of the black masses in recent years as has Malcolm X. It is not precisely what he said—Malcolm called himself "flexible" and his views did shift from time to time—so much as the spirit or mood he conveyed. It is a moot question whether Malcolm was a product of the vast subterranean unrest that had been seething among the Northern urban Negro masses since the early years of the great migration, or whether he pounced upon the despair and frustration of the ghetto streets and fashioned it in his own image. One suspects a little of both. He was successful because he expressed in language his people could understand the feelings they seldom dared articulate even to

themselves. He had the effrontery not only to "tell it the
way it is" to Negroes but, more astonishingly, to their
white liberal friends. He served therefore as a fiery symbol
of black anger and courage for millions, openly or covertly
—even for those who did not necessarily agree with everything he said. He was, above all, a teacher and minister
(like his father before him), passionately devoted to his
flock—the poor, the dispossessed, the pariahs, the menials
—and he made them feel a dignity and pride they had
never before experienced. He was clearly a man in search
of himself and his destiny. The tortuous paths he took
were fraught with pitfalls, agony, and self-deception, and
he died far from his intended goals. But he died his own
man at least, and in his death he bequeathed a legacy of
unfinished history.

Since his death in 1965, two remarkable books have
appeared. The first, an autobiography, he had been preparing the last couple of years of his life with the assistance of a journalist, Alex Haley. The second, *Malcolm X
Speaks*, is a compilation of some of the speeches, radio
broadcasts, and other public statements he delivered in
roughly the same period of time. Each complements the
other in revealing the character of the man and his ideas.
Strictly speaking, neither of these works is "literary," if by
literary one means that Malcolm deliberately sat down
and wrote the words. In the first case he talked about his
life to Haley, who transcribed his words verbatim and
then, presumably, structured them into chapters. Haley in
turn resubmitted them for Malcolm's approval. According
to Haley, the corrections and changes were negligible. The
entire tone of the book is informal, colloquial—that of a
man speaking directly to his audience.

In the course of his two years with Haley, Malcolm
severed his connections with Elijah Muhammad's Black
Muslim movement and struck out on his own. Hence ap-
proximately seventy per cent of the book is told from
Malcolm's zealous Black Muslim orientation, the remaining thirty per cent from a more independent existential

standpoint. Haley feared that after the break with Muhammad Malcolm would want to rewrite the first part as an embittered polemic against the Muslims—but Malcolm agreed to allow the words to stand as they were originally spoken.

The tone of *Malcolm X Speaks* is hardly distinguishable from that of the autobiography. The public Malcolm and the private Malcolm sound very nearly like the same person. In part, of course, this can be explained by the fact that Malcolm never wrote out his speeches beforehand but spoke spontaneously from notes. (Most of the speeches included in the book have been taken from tapes.) Both books therefore possess the informal, improvised quality of Malcolm's voice, and this coincidence of tone suggests a reason for the magnetic quality of the man. His listeners must have sensed that Malcolm gave very nearly all of himself when he addressed them. He never talked down to his audience. When he taught—and his speeches are full of parables and lessons—Malcolm was teaching himself at the same time. One feels that his insights might have dawned upon him the day before, and that he was bursting to share them with someone.

Malcolm was no ordinary thinker, nor was he really an extraordinary one. From the relatively simplistic racist and separatist outlook of his Black Muslim period, he moved toward a somewhat socialistic world view at the time of his death. Far from being Machiavellian or calculating, as many of his admirers and enemies have contended, Malcolm's inconsistencies and reversals may be better comprehended in terms of his augmented understanding. Frequently, some rankling feeling would rise to the fore and he would say things in a burst of anger that he came to rue afterwards. On these occasions, Malcolm would contradict himself several times within the same speech—sometimes in the same breath. It was usually his more violent racist sentiments that caught the headlines— even after he had "reformed"—allowing sanctimonious editorial writers to say he was still a reverse racist and a menace to improved race relations. Like the white press, some civil rights organizations and black nationalist groups, who have invoked Malcolm as their patron saint, are all convinced they have caught the authentic voice of Malcolm—and in a manner of speaking each of them is right. Malcolm's specific views were seldom fixed for very long.

A careful reading of both these books does, nonetheless, suggest that Malcolm was moving, however erratically, in a direction that in some cases transcended or bypassed, or indeed rejected, some of the statements he himself had uttered at one time or another. It would be foolhardy to attempt to formulate Malcolm into doctrine or dogma; his very spirit was growth and searching. One can only speculate where he might have ended had he lived; one imagines, however, that he would be as hard to pin down alive as he is dead.

No public figure in recent memory has lived his own philosophy so intensely. As a hustler on the streets of Harlem, believing that all of life was a gigantic confidence game, he worked feverishly at his underworld career—as he did later as a missionary for Elijah Muhammad's Black Muslim movement. So zealously did he proselytize that he brought Muhammad's small cult of four hundred members, centered mostly in the Midwest, to a nationwide enterprise of forty thousand well-publicized, militant Negroes.

Later, when he broke with the Muslims and sought further to deepen his religious understanding, he journeyed alone to Mecca where he underwent a conversion to orthodox Islam. (Paradoxically, it was his experiences in feudal Saudi Arabia rather than in democratic America that tended to erase Malcolm's racist feelings.) Finally, when he determined that the Negro's struggle for freedom in America required international support, Malcolm lobbied with African heads of state on visits he made to Africa. He had begun to achieve some results when he was gunned down at a Harlem rally in February, 1965. He was thirty-nine.

Some of the facts of Malcolm's early life are so little known that it is essential to rehearse them. He was born Malcolm Little, the fourth of nine children of his father's second marriage, in Omaha in 1925. His mother was a light-skinned West Indian, his father an itinerant Baptist preacher who preached the black nationalism of Marcus Garvey's back-to-Africa movement. Shortly after Malcolm's birth, the Reverend Little, responding to threats by the Ku Klux Klan, removed his family to Milwaukee, and then to East Lansing, Michigan, where he resumed his nationalist activities as a visiting preacher at various Negro churches in the area. A local vigilante group known as the Black Legionnaires attacked the Little home in the dead of night and burned it to the ground while the police and fire department looked on passively. With his own hands the Reverend Little built a new house on the outskirts of East Lansing. When Malcolm was six, his father was run down by a trolley. The police called it an accident, but local Negroes whispered that he was murdered by white racists.

The family began gradually to disintegrate. Malcolm's mother, a proud woman, submitted to welfare, and Malcolm describes in bitter detail the humiliations she had to undergo at the hands of social workers. In 1937 she was committed to a state mental institution, and the impoverished and hungry children were distributed among various families in the vicinity. Malcolm did not remain long in the home in which he was placed. His deportment in school was evidently regarded as rebellious, and the courts remanded him to a detention home in Mason, Michigan—a sort of halfway house to reform school. The home was run by a benign but patronizing white couple, and here for a while Malcolm flourished. He attended junior high school in town and performed at the top of his class each year. He was relatively popular with his white classmates, played basketball on the school team, and when he was in the seventh grade he was elected class president.

A turning point came the following year, when a

teacher asked Malcolm what he intended to do with his life. When he said he would like to become a lawyer, the teacher responded that this was an unrealistic goal for a "nigger," that he would be wiser if he planned to do something with his hands, perhaps become a carpenter. Upon graduation from junior high school, Malcolm left Michigan to live with his half sister, Ella, in Boston.

Malcolm's Michigan years take up only two chapters of his entire autobiography, and yet they are the most moving and provocative, for they suggest many of the elements of his later career. What, after all, could be more pathetic than the smashed innocence of childhood, the abrupt and brutal separation from one's loved ones, the first terrifying confrontations with the evils of racism? But the pathos of his account lies in the manner in which he tells it. Malcolm focuses for the most part on events, without attempting to interpret, moralize, or analyze. His story is charged with its own meaning, and Malcolm well knows it. Perhaps if he were to dwell too long on his emotional associations, he would find them intolerable. At one point he tells Haley:

> I have rarely talked to anyone about my mother, for I believe that I am capable of killing a person, without hesitation, who happened to make the wrong kind of remark about my mother. So I purposely don't make any opening for some fool to step into.

Malcolm's narrative resembles the classic textbook prognosis of an irretrievable delinquent and hardened criminal—a milieu of poverty, family and social tensions, omnipresent threats of violence, constant shifts and movement from one locality to another, the early absence of a strong masculine figure upon whom Malcolm could depend and model himself, a distressingly disoriented mother who would not or could not lavish much love on him. And his later activities in Boston and Harlem fulfill such an evaluation.

But though all the clinical observations work themselves out satisfactorily, on a deeper level they prove as well something altogether different. However much Malcolm may have missed him, his father undoubtedly made a strong impression. Indeed, Malcolm's life more and more appeared to mirror that of his father up until the time of his death. Both expressed impassioned religious zeal in their defiance of the white man; both took pride in themselves as Negroes and in their African heritage; and both endeavored to bring Africa to American Negroes directly. Strangest of all, both anticipated death by violence with considerable accuracy. Perhaps in a way they invited death as a happy surcease from their frenzied struggles. To die in the service of what he believed, Malcolm says in his autobiography, was a fate he expected, and several times he told Haley he did not expect to live long enough to read it. Malcolm's father died in similar fashion, in similar "service." Malcolm recalls the tensions that existed between his parents just prior to his father's death—how his mother one day pleaded with her husband not to leave for town but how he insisted he must, and how they both must have known instinctively he would not return.

Rather than weaken him, possibly the adversity Malcolm suffered as a child inured him to the shock and betrayals he knew as an adult. This is not to suggest that the scars were not real, permanent, or tragic; yet one wonders how someone not seasoned in Malcolm's peculiar kind of hell would have fared under the conditions he knew later as a man. Malcolm's "racial" attitudes, for example, may be understood not simply in terms of the color war into which he was born—here it was simply black against white—but perhaps more painfully in terms of his parents' attitude toward him. He suspects that his militantly nationalistic father, whom he adored, favored him because he had light skin, and that his "white" mother subconsciously rejected him for the same reason. She "would tell me to get out of the house and 'Let the sun shine on you so you can get some color.'" Surely Mal-

colm's racial ambivalencies—even after he had returned
from Mecca a believer in the brotherhood of men of all
colors—may be partially understood in terms of the con-
fusion he felt as a child.

Additionally, Malcolm's puritanical sexual values may
be attributed to the same source. His first "real" girl
friend, prior to his going to jail, was a white girl with
whom he had a libertine affair that continued even after
she married. The anger Malcolm frequently vented on
Sophia could not have been too dissimilar to his feelings
about his "white" mother. "It seems that some women
love to be exploited. When they are not exploited, they
exploit the man. . . . Always, every now and then, I had
given her a hard time, just to keep her in line. Every once
in a while, a woman seems to need, in fact *wants* this,
too." After Malcolm's conversion to the Black Muslim
faith he renounced his loose sexual past, and he maintained the strictest abstinence in his relations with women
until he married. Even then he continued to regard
them—especially white women—as seductive, untrustworthy, and potentially emasculating.

> I'd had too much experience that women were only
> tricky, deceitful, untrustworthy flesh. I had seen too many
> men ruined, or at least tied down, or in some other way
> messed up by women. Women talked too much. To tell a
> woman not to talk too much was like telling Jesse James
> not to carry a gun, or telling a hen not to cackle. Can you
> imagine Jesse James without a gun, or a hen that didn't
> cackle?

Even after breaking with Elijah Muhammad, Malcolm
could say this about the semi-Westernized women he saw
in Lebanon:

> . . . my attention was struck by the mannerisms and
> attire of the Lebanese women. In the Holy Land, there
> had been the very modest, very feminine Arabian women
> —and there was this sudden contrast of the half-French,
> half-Arab Lebanese women who projected in their dress
> and street manners more liberty, more boldness. I saw

clearly the obvious European influence upon the Lebanese culture. It showed me how any country's moral strength, or its moral weakness, is quickly measurable by the street attire and attitude of its women—especially its young women. . . . Witness the women, both young and old, in America—where scarcely any moral values are left.

Malcolm well understood as an adult that racial and sexual attitudes were interrelated, and that the Negro could never achieve his freedom until he had straightened out his feelings about his manhood. He understood that oppression of the Negro robbed him of his masculinity, his pride in himself, and his sense of dignity—and in his speeches Malcolm constantly harps on this theme. As a boy in Mason, Michigan, he was constantly made to feel his inadequacies. In his history class the teacher made fun of the Negro's contribution and told "nigger" jokes, and when he attended school dances with the basketball team he was attuned to the psychic message that it was taboo to dance with white girls. He recalls how his white male classmates revealed to him sexual intimacies, as if Malcolm, being a Negro and hence a primitive, would somehow know all about these things. He speaks of attending the movie *Gone with the Wind*, in which the Negro maid acted so obsequiously that he wanted to "crawl." The cultural cues, sometimes subtle, sometimes inadvertent, sometimes unconscious, but always implying the subhuman nature of the Negro, challenge and destroy his virility. Possibly Malcolm's insistence that women keep their place was motivated in part by a nagging insecurity about his own manhood—but even more significantly, he must have known that if Negro women were properly subordinated, their men might gain support for their injured egos.

The most intriguing parts of the autobiography are those which deal with Malcolm's experiences just before he acquired fame. It is not simply that the lurid life he led in Boston and Harlem shocks complacent middle-class readers—the culture of the poor always seems foreign—

but that Malcolm tells it with such zest that he
almost belies his penitence. He describes his arrival in
Boston looking "like a hick," his education on the streets
and in the poolrooms and dance halls, his jitterbug phase
and the zoot suits he wore, his girl friends, white and
Negro, his strong-willed half sister Ella, and his guide and
mentor in the ways of the streets, Shorty. Although Ella
would have liked him to associate with middle-class and
respectable Negroes, Malcolm felt more at ease with the
poor, since they at least had no illusions about their status
in American society, and throughout the book he excoriates the black bourgeoisie for being the deluded instruments white men use in controlling the black masses.
(Among these he includes most civil rights leaders—and
he names many of them in his speeches.)

Malcolm does not, however, altogether exclude the
black masses from much of his scorn, since they exhibit
disturbing manifestations of self-hatred. One of the most
egregious of these is "conking." Malcolm was initiated
into this rite by his friend Shorty. It is an extremely long,
involved and painful process of straightening the hair.
By so doing, Malcolm observes, Negroes are expressing
hatred for their Negroid characteristics, and here lies the
principal barrier to their regeneration. White society has
so invested Negroes with a sense of being unworthy and
despised that they even attempt to *look* like white men.

Malcolm's greatest message as a teacher—both within
and outside the Black Muslim movement—was that Negroes must acquire a sense of dignity, a sense of personal
pride and value in their identity. All the civil rights legislation in the world—and he had little use for any of it—
would not do one iota of good until Negroes themselves
transformed their self-defeating concepts of themselves.

Any understanding of Malcolm's political, social, economic and religious views must take this into account. At
the base of all his pronouncements, despite his shifts and
reversals, Malcolm stood first for the psychological redemption of Negroes. It was chiefly for this reason that he

attained such an enormous following among the seemingly apathetic and despairing masses of the American cities. He struck first at the heart—arousing wonder in his listeners at the depths and complexities of their own feelings—and then only secondarily at the world they never made.

Malcolm left Boston for New York when he was sixteen. He worked as a sandwich salesman on the Yankee Clipper, an afternoon express train between New York and Boston, and then as a waiter at Small's Paradise Bar, a well-known cocktail lounge and restaurant in Harlem. It was at Small's that he met numbers racketeers, pimps, narcotics peddlers, and a variety of other underworld types. The old-timers told him the story of the Negro in New York, a history that dates back to colonial times. What appalled him, Malcolm said afterward, was the ignorance of both whites and Negroes regarding the role Negroes have played in American history.

In a sense, Small's was Malcolm's first awakening. There is genuine delight in his account of some of the customers, and he describes in loving detail their characteristics and various "hustles." But what moved him most was the camaraderie and warmth that pervaded the atmosphere. For the first time in many years Malcolm found haven and security—albeit among thieves whose very existence stood constantly threatened. Again and again, he speaks of the essential irony of their situation.

> Many times since, I have thought about it, and what it really meant. In one sense, we were huddled in there, bonded together in seeking security and warmth and comfort from each other, and we didn't know it. All of us— who might have probed space, or cured cancer, or built industries—were, instead, black victims of the white man's American social system.

Malcolm was dismissed from Small's when it was discovered that he had directed a soldier to the home of a prostitute. The soldier, an Army spy, informed authorities who in turn might have revoked Small's license.

Malcolm's next two years were given over to criminal
activities. In order to survive in Harlem, he says, he had
to discover some kind of hustle. Everyone did. He sold
narcotics (and used them), he bootlegged, he pimped, he
gambled, he worked for numbers racketeers, and he re-
sorted finally to armed robbery to maintain his "high
style" of living. The pages describing his Harlem years are
rich in incident and anecdote. Malcolm apparently attempted every conceivable hustle. Seldom has the fringe
underworld life of Harlem been treated so extensively.
Yet in dealing with this period Malcolm does not record
events dispassionately. His language is fraught with moral
expletives, condemnations of self—and perhaps, above
all, the first clear articulations in his own mind of anti-
white attitudes. At one juncture in his career he steered
rich, powerful white men to Negro prostitutes.

> I got my first schooling about the cesspool morals of the
> white man from the best possible source, from his own
> women. And then as I got deeper into my own life of evil,
> I saw the white man's morals with my own eyes. I even
> made my living helping to guide him to the sick things he
> wanted.

But Malcolm is not without humor, and he takes considerable pleasure in telling how he evaded the draft. He
arrived for his physical examination wearing an extreme
zoot suit, "skipping and tipping, and I thrust my tattered
Greetings at that reception desk's white soldier—'Crazy-
o, daddy-o, get me moving. I can't wait to get in that
brown—'" He made such a spectacle of himself that he
was ultimately sent to a psychiatrist. After a few quiet
questions,

> Suddenly, I sprang up and peeped under both doors, the
> one I'd entered and another that probably was a closet.
> And then I bent and whispered fast in his ear. "Daddy-o,
> now you and me, we're from up North here, so don't you
> tell nobody. . . . I want to get sent down South. Organize
> them nigger soldiers, you dig? Steal us some guns, and
> kill up crackers!"

That psychiatrist's blue pencil dropped, and his professional manner fell off in all directions. He stared at me as if I were a snake's egg hatching, fumbling for his red pencil. I knew I had him. I was going back out . . . when he said, "That will be all."

Malcolm's Harlem hustling career was short-lived. At the end of two years he discovered himself being pursued by a Harlem numbers racketeer, Italian gangsters, and the police. He retreated to Boston, where, after a short respite, he organized a burglary ring consisting of Shorty, Sophia and her younger sister, and a third young man whom Shorty knew. Malcolm was apprehended pawning a stolen watch, and the entire group was brought to trial. Malcolm and Shorty got eight to ten years; the girls were given considerably shorter sentences. Malcolm was convinced the inordinate length of his sentence was the result of his association with white girls. He was nineteen.

In the literature of religious conversion there is probably nothing more remarkable than Malcolm's account of his assumption of the Black Muslim faith. His conversion came, appropriately enough, in Norfolk Prison Colony, where he had time to consider the chaos of his life. But the stages by which he achieved conversion deserve the attention of students of the phenomenon. He entered prison in the blackest of moods. So incorrigible, nasty, and angry was he that his prison mates nicknamed him "Satan," and he was delivered often to solitary confinement.

I preferred the solitary that this behavior brought me. I would pace for hours like a caged leopard, viciously cursing aloud to myself. And my favorite targets were the Bible and God.

His nihilism was occasioned in part by the absence of drugs, in part by the very wretchedness of the prison—it was built in 1805.

Any person who claims to have deep feeling for other human beings should think a long, long time before he votes to have other men kept behind bars—caged. I am not saying there shouldn't be prisons, but there shouldn't be bars. Behind bars, a man never reforms. He will never forget. He never will get completely over the memory of the bars.

The extremes of Malcolm's disposition appear to have prepared him for complete submission to father surrogates. The first of these was a convict named Bimbi. According to Malcolm, Bimbi commanded the complete respect of the prison inmates by virtue of his vast knowledge and intelligence. Bimbi observed that Malcolm had untapped potential, and Malcolm set about modeling himself on Bimbi's example.

Bimbi advised him to take prison correspondence courses and use the prison library, and Malcolm devoted untold hours to his reading and self-education. He particularly loved history and linguistics, and he relates with almost embarrassing schoolboy pride the discoveries he made. A world had opened up for him, and if Malcolm at times sounds naïve and parades his learning, it should be remembered that his education took place in a milieu not altogether suited to the academic style. One cannot help noting as well, however, that some of his insights were shrewd and might never have been drawn had he educated himself in more conventional fashion.

Malcolm's curriculum was of his own choosing, and some of his methods are almost beyond belief. He determined one day to enlarge his vocabulary and so he took to transcribing all the words in the dictionary. Long before his prison term had ended, he succeeded. Years afterward, Malcolm told Haley how much he regretted his lack of formal education—how, indeed, he would have liked to become a lawyer and engage in dialectics with intellectual equals. The audiences he liked most to address, next to the black masses, were college audiences. They stimulated him.

Second only to his father, the most momentous figure in Malcolm's life was Elijah Muhammad, whose teachings

Malcolm's family introduced him to. So much of Elijah's doctrine is fantastic (he taught, for example, that the white man is an aberrant species of Negro whose genes had been artificially grafted by a diabolical scientist, Mr. Yacub, some six thousand years ago) that one wonders how anyone could take him seriously. But especially among Negro convicts—whom the Muslims were recruiting successfully—he reached men sunk in the depths of despair and articulated for them how badly off they were. He smashed away at illusions and then proceeded to construct an identity out of their bare consciousness. A sense of identity emerges from feeling—and the feelings Elijah most successfully aroused were those of unabashed hatred. The elements were all there to begin with—Elijah did not create them. He told the convicts that they were oppressed and exploited and ravaged by white men for centuries, that they were descendants of a proud civilization, that they did not even know their true African names since the white man had robbed them of these, too—and then he asked all who read his message to re-examine their own lives, in the light of their experiences with white men, to see if it were not true that they had always been maltreated by whites.

For Malcolm, as for many others, it all seemed to fit. Everything he knew, everything he had been reading about the history of the white man's treatment of darker people, had been confirmed. What did it matter that Muslim theology, cosmogony, history, politics appeared absurd? What could be more absurd than what had happened to the black man? If Elijah struck at the deeper, essential poetic truths, then everything else he taught must surely have been true as well. In later years Malcolm preached in the same pattern. First he would reduce his listeners to a sense of their own abjectness. Then almost at the same time he would give them a sense of themselves by awakening an articulate anger directed outward to the source of their misery—the white man.

Muhammad demanded of his followers an absolute discipline as regards dogma, ritual, dietary laws, dress, and moral comportment. He stripped them of their Christian surnames as shameful vestiges of their benighted history. As arduous as these sacrifices may have been, they brought his followers a clarity about their own identity— an identity they never before knew existed.

Malcolm Little, the convict, the former Harlem hustler, was utterly persuaded. He struggled against belief, but succumbed one night in a vision of Elijah sitting quietly and protectively next to him in his cell. Malcolm whispered to his Negro prison mates that the white man was the devil, and that he already worshiped and adored Elijah Muhammed although he had yet to meet him. He was saved.

Malcolm's career in the service of Elijah Muhammad is a matter of public record. After leaving prison, he rejoined his brothers in Detroit and became a member of the Detroit temple. He met Elijah shortly thereafter—they had corresponded while Malcolm was still in prison—and Elijah tutored Malcolm in his home in the further tenets of the faith. Malcolm's narration of their early relationship is replete with endearments. His gratitude to Elijah was boundless; he was like a father for whom Malcolm would gladly have given his life. Elijah ordained Malcolm a minister, and so impassioned was he before his small Detroit congregation that Elijah later allowed him to proselytize the faith on a nation-wide basis.

Long afterward, Malcolm told Haley that whatever differences existed between the two men lay in the direction of Malcolm's zeal. Malcolm, having attained absolute truth, wanted to spread the word as rapidly and indiscriminately as possible, but Elijah restrained him, cautioning him against precipitous action that might endanger the movement.

Malcolm's account of his missionary endeavors in Harlem is instructive. He was not particularly successful in persuading Negroes to join the movement in street corner addresses. He was regarded simply as another orator for the bewildering variety of urban fringe organizations that vie for the Negro's attention. The Muslims enjoyed better fortune "fishing" for new members along the edge of nationalist street corner meetings, and especially among Christian store-front churches. Malcolm and his cohorts would wait in the streets until the termination of services, and then pass among the emerging congregations, informing them that the truth had at last been discovered and inviting them to attend a Muslim gathering. Evidently Malcolm's electrifying message—and manner of delivery —met with better success among the dispirited and alienated elements who sought solace in evangelism. Malcolm would inveigh against Christianity as the white man's instrument of repression. He taught that heaven existed only on earth, that it was attainable if only black men had the strength of character to seize it. Elijah was undoubtedly impressed by Malcolm's success. He may also have begun to worry whether Malcolm's image was surpassing his own.

It is doubtful whether Malcolm would have come so quickly to the attention of the white public were it not for the fiery message of "violence" he preached. His emergence on the national scene occurred at a time of well-publicized integration demonstrations, Southern violence, and Congressional deliberations on civil rights legislation. But everything Malcolm seemed to be saying was antithetical to the most progressive trends. In actuality he was simply echoing the ghetto's not-so-silent conviction that the Negro ought to meet violence with violence. Malcolm was pictured in the press as a dangerous demagogue for having expressed in words what everyone knew.

He was first of all a racist who termed all whites devils —at a time when more whites than ever before were actively participating in the civil rights movement. But Malcolm insisted that the white man was responsible for the black man's agony and that forgiveness was impossible. Secondly, Malcolm called for an independent Negro state. He called integration a gigantic fraud perpetrated by "devils" who had no intention of keeping their promises. When Malcolm was accused of advocating segregation in reverse, he responded that segregation implied outside control of the black community by whites. His goal was complete separation, a state utterly in control of its own politics and economy. He pointed with pride to Black Muslim schools and businesses which endowed their participants with a sense of their own worth. He spoke to Haley of the Muslims' immense success in redeeming narcotics addicts and criminals. If Malcolm possessed only the haziest notion of government and economic theory, of the pragmatic manner in which his (or more properly speaking, Elijah's) program was to be carried out, he struck the deeper truth that the regeneration of the depressed Negro must stem from his own inner resources—and that this implied, radical as it may sound, the exclusion of whites. In the late fifties and early sixties, he hammered away at these themes. He addressed black audiences the country over and appeared on national radio and television programs. His views were requested by a wide variety of college audiences.

The break with Elijah was probably inevitable. By 1963 he had far eclipsed Elijah as a national figure, and his aggressive campaign on behalf of the Muslim movement could not have suited Elijah's more cautious approach. Jealousies were bound to occur; rumor had it that Elijah wanted one of his sons to succeed him as head of the church and that he feared Malcolm's domination of the movement. Elijah began to curb Malcolm's public appearances on mass media, and his name was seldom mentioned in the Muslim newspaper, *Muhammad Speaks*. When Malcolm learned that Elijah had allegedly committed adultery, he was horrified. Elijah, Malcolm says, attempted to gloss over the whole affair privately with him, but Malcolm's faith was badly shaken. Shortly thereafter, Elijah publicly "silenced" Malcolm for ninety days for having transgressed Elijah's command banning any public statement about President Kennedy's assassination.

(Malcolm had said at a rally that it was simply a case of the "chickens coming home to roost," which out of context sounds cruel, but which Malcolm insisted only meant that a violent civilization destroyed one of its own leaders.) Malcolm accepted Elijah's command sullenly, but then he learned, he said, from one of his lieutenants in the Harlem mosque, that Elijah had declared he wanted Malcolm dead.

Malcolm did not await the end of his ninety-day humiliation; he announced to the press the establishment of an independent Harlem mosque, with himself at the head, which all Negroes of any faith could join. It would be dedicated to the Negro's fight for freedom and would work alongside civil rights groups.

Elijah's betrayal struck Malcolm very hard. He arranged with his half sister, Ella, for money to undertake a pilgrimage to Mecca to restore himself spiritually. He came under the influence of Dr. Abd ir-Rahman Azzam, an Islamic scholar and official in the Saudi Arabian government. Malcolm seems to have transferred all his affection from Elijah to his new mentor—and presumably it was Dr. Azzam's approval and encouragement that helped liberate Malcolm for his new role. He now, one imagines, came to regard himself as unofficial visiting ambassador from the American ghettos. He toured a large number of African countries addressing religious, political, and intellectual audiences everywhere about the "criminal" racist conditions in the United States. But Malcolm's own racial views had changed considerably in the process. What impressed him most about his Near East pilgrimage, he said, was the equality and brotherhood of persons of all colors in their search for God. It was this image he took home with him and which he cherished most until his death.

Malcolm's subsequent political and social thinking is best developed for the reader in the 1964–65 collection of speeches, *Malcolm X Speaks*. By this time Malcolm may have lost some of his power over the black masses, but he appears more independent and his views more sophisticated. He still stood first of all for the militant defense of Negro rights. The black man, he averred, would never achieve his self-respect and sense of manhood until he stopped allowing himself to be beaten by white racists at civil rights demonstrations. On one occasion he called for an organization of terrorists like the Kenya Mau Mau who would enter Mississippi and avenge the deaths of Negro and white civil rights workers. In this respect he was still considerably at odds with most civil rights groups, who continued to call for passive resistance. (At this writing organizations like CORE and SNCC have begun advocating positions similar to Malcolm's.) But Malcolm insisted that history revealed that the most successful attempts at freedom were won only by groups who fought actively and physically for their rights. If white oppressors opposed Negroes peacefully, it would be an altogether different matter, but under present conditions in the South and elsewhere it was the sheerest madness to invite death without fighting back.

He scorned the so-called Negro Revolution. A revolution, he said, implied the overturn of a political, social, and economic system. What was actually happening was that Negroes were attempting to integrate themselves into a system *designed* to oppress them. The only possible beneficiaries were a few of the Negro bourgeoisie, who were utterly out of touch with the needs and the sentiments of the urban black masses. He now regarded socialism—whose workings he saw in Egypt and other African countries—as one of the principal means of achieving equality. He also called for the "internationalization" of the freedom struggle. It was no longer, he said, a matter of civil rights, but rather one of "human rights." The black man had been so inhumanely oppressed by white Americans for centuries that the time had come for other nations whose colored peoples constituted the great majority of the world population to protest vigorously the treatment of their brothers. America's domestic and foreign policies were in reality one and the same, he said. What was happening in Mississippi had an equivalent meaning in terms of American actions in Vietnam, China, Cuba, the Congo, and among Afro-Asian peoples generally. (If Malcolm's accusations appear simplistic, it may well be that he struck at a deeper truth than he realized. The United States and Western European nations have always moved more quickly to defend their "interests" among colored peoples in Africa and Asia than they have among Caucasian countries.)

Malcolm claimed that the exploitation of minority peoples in America was, after all, the mirror image of American colonial exploitation abroad. Insofar as Malcolm now saw the Negro struggle in terms of a wider global problem, he requested Afro-Asian leaders to submit their support in the United Nations and through other appropriate channels. To this end, upon his return from Mecca, he created his Organization of Afro-American Unity, whose purpose would be to unify all Negro rights groups and relate them culturally and politically to similar anticolonial movements abroad. In keeping with Malcolm's general views of self-help, he insisted that only Negroes join his organization, although whites might help provide support financially.

More significant than his words were his actions. Malcolm went to Africa a second time in 1964, visiting a number of countries to rally support for his views among African leaders and intellectuals. Again he was met everywhere as a celebrity, and apparently was making some inroads. The State Department expressed concern. In February, 1965, Malcolm flew to Paris to address a gathering of African students. A large crush of people assembled at the airport to greet him, but French officials barred his entry without explanation and forced Malcolm to turn back. He had clearly become an international "menace." Before the end of the month, he was assassinated at a rally in Harlem.

What manner of man was Malcolm? There is always the temptation to idealize a figure who has died a martyr for his ideals. And there can never be any question about Malcolm's courage or his sincerity. But the person who emerges from these books is neither a Greek hero nor a calculating demagogue. Despite his revolutionary ardor and the extreme—often exotic—vagaries of his fortunes, he sounds like nothing so much as the quintessential American. Consider, for example, his pragmatism. Regardless of the "orthodoxy" he may at any moment have been espousing, Malcolm relied chiefly upon his own personal experiences to arrive at any conclusion he drew. If doctrine conformed to what he personally felt to be true, then Malcolm appeared to be unswerving in his devotion, but if, conversely, experience belied doctrine, Malcolm would sometimes, unknown to himself, diverge from strict adherence and strike out on his own tack.

On one occasion he tells Haley he knows integration cannot work because he tried it himself as a boy in Mason, Michigan. Later on, he says that when he began in 1963 to doubt Elijah Muhammad in his own mind, he found himself inadvertently stressing social views more and more to the exclusion of theology. Throughout both books he constantly illustrates his points with homespun adages drawn from his ghetto experiences, parallels with his own life, or down-to-earth parables that touch on the direct knowledge of his audience. His language is always simple, straightforward, often colloquial and without the slightest trace of condescension. He constantly exhorts his audiences to think for themselves, to discover for themselves if what he has to say is not right.

Here is a portion of an address he delivered to a delegation of Mississippi youth in Harlem in 1964.

> One of the first things I think young people, especially nowadays, should learn is how to see for yourself and listen for yourself and think for yourself. Then you can come to an intelligent decision for yourself. . . . If you don't do it, you'll always be maneuvered into a situation

where you are never fighting your actual enemies, where you will find yourself fighting your own self.

I think our people in this country are the best examples of that. Many of us want to be nonviolent. Here in Harlem, where there are probably more black people concentrated than any place in the world, some talk that nonviolent talk too. But we find that they aren't nonviolent with each other. You can go out to Harlem Hospital, where there are more black patients than any hospital in the world, and see them going in there all cut up and shot up and busted up where they got violent with each other.

My experience has been that in many instances where you find Negroes talking about nonviolence, they are not nonviolent with each other, and they're not loving with each other, or forgiving with each other. Usually when they say they're nonviolent, they mean they're nonviolent with somebody else.

Malcolm reveals his American character in other ways as well. Like an inveterate frontier Calvinist, once he feels he has discovered the truth he plunges heedlessly and enthusiastically ahead in order to fulfill God's will. Elijah Muhammad had trouble restraining him—and here is Malcolm after his conversion to orthodox Islam in Mecca:

Behind my nods and smiles, though, I was doing some American-type thinking and reflection. I saw that Islam's conversions around the world could double and triple if the colorfulness and the true spiritualness of the Hajj pilgrimage were properly advertised and communicated to the outside world. I saw that the Arabs are poor at understanding the psychology of non-Arabs and the importance of public relations. The Arabs said "insha Allah" ("God willing")—then they waited for converts. Even by this means, Islam was on the march, but I knew that with improved public relations methods the number of new converts turning to Allah could be turned into millions.

There was a booster quality about Malcolm, an enthusiasm and aggressiveness that was at once democratically engaging and embarrassingly naïve.

Nor did Malcolm fail to partake of the typical American's disdain for pomp and high places while wallowing in gratitude at the honors bestowed on him from the same sources. He could approach world leaders without the faintest modesty, while simultaneously experiencing humility and reverence in their presence. Malcolm's air of astonishment and awe that he should be received so graciously at a Harvard Law School forum or King Faisal's court is sometimes a little hard to take. Yet considering his origins and his meteoric rise to fame, such feelings are understandable. Finally, Malcolm's innate distrust of government and outside interference in the affairs of men, and his consequent faith in the capacity of individuals to elevate themselves by virtue of their own powers, is undoubtedly one of the oldest American traditions (or prejudices) of them all. Was not his own life a rather nightmarish rags-to-riches myth?

What raised Malcolm above the common herd of men was his immense compassion for his people and his almost fanatic sense of being called to the role he was expected to play. He was often bigoted, ignorant, and misinformed—yet he possessed the malleability to grow and learn. He was the best and worst of Americans. He might have made a great leader.

Chapter IX

The Expatriate as Novelist: William Demby

Since the 1920's, a considerable number of Negro authors have gone abroad to live and work. Some have returned, dissatisfied and weary at what they have found. But a surprising hard core have remained overseas, determined, in one way or another, to fashion a better life for themselves. As Negroes, they say, they are made constantly aware of their status in America, and race consciousness cannot help but influence the character of their work. Here, then, they write as Negroes first and artists second; hopefully, in a "raceless" milieu they might avoid such difficulties.

Unfortunately, in the vast majority of cases, they do not succeed. Unlike such

white writers as James, Hemingway, Eliot, Pound, Fitzgerald, and the others who managed to assimilate their
foreign experiences, most Negro authors find they cannot
use their new environment. And seldom do they attempt
to do so. They revert to American backgrounds again and
again in each succeeding work they write.

Nor have they fared much better in discovering the
"objectivity" they sought. Instead, paradoxically, they
write with an increasing bitterness, coupled with a sense
of life that no longer seems to ring quite true. Their failure may, of course, be attributed to their individual capa-
bilities. But undoubtedly the underlying cause is not—as
has so often been charged—that they have severed their
roots, but that they had no deep American roots to begin
with. One and all, they have protested, with considerable
justification, that as Negroes they could find no meaningful place in American life—that they have been excluded
and despised, and as a result they have sought an outlet
for their creative energies elsewhere. But how could they
hope to succeed in an environment still more foreign than
the one they have known?

One remarkable exception is the novelist William
Demby. Demby's works reveal a thoroughly unself-con-
scious immersion in European modes of thinking, conditioned by a profoundly American outlook. He is, like his
literary ancestors, Melville and Hawthorne, obsessed with
the problem of evil, but he expresses his concerns in philosophical terms akin to Christian existentialism. He has
appropriated techniques ranging from Joycean stream of
consciousness to modern cinematography, and incorpor-
ated these as instruments of his philosophical quest.

There is little about his early life that distinguishes him
as a promising American author. He was born in 1922
and grew up in Pittsburgh and Clarksburg, West Virginia,
a coal-mining region where his father occupied a minor
executive position for an oil company. He attended West
Virginia State College and then served in the cavalry and
as a reporter for *Stars and Stripes* in Italy during World

War II. After the war he returned to Fisk University, where he participated in student publications, writing short stories and reviews, and illustrating and designing the college magazine. He went back to Italy for graduate work in art history at the University of Rome in 1947, and later worked as a journalist and as a translator and writer for the Italian television and film industries.

In 1950, he published his first novel, *Beetlecreek*, which garnered some critical success but very little public attention. Demby's career as a screen writer took him on various occasions to other parts of the world, but he lived mainly in Rome with his Italian wife and Italian-born son. After spending nearly a third of his life abroad, he returned to the United States late in 1963. Two years afterward, his second novel, *The Catacombs*, was published.

Such meager biographical data can scarcely provide any major insights into Demby's creative psychology. What does become apparent, however, are the obvious extremes of his experiences. He was brought up in the relatively confining atmosphere of the Negro ghettos of Pittsburgh and a West Virginia mining town. Even as a college student, he attended all-Negro institutions. As an adult, on the other hand, living a cosmopolitan life among film directors, writers, artists, and the like, his life assumes an altogether different character. These opposing patterns are reflected in his work, where they are pitted against one another as the central conflict of his novels.

In a very real sense the drama in Demby's works revolves around an ever-shifting battle between Life and Death. Death, or evil, is equated with the static, the inert, the stultifying qualities of existence—and judging from the allusions in his works to his American years, one would gather Demby regards this period as having been deadly and constraining. Life, for its part, implies creative evolutionary energies, love and reason. These, presumably, Demby discovered in the European phases of his career.

Although its setting is a small Negro community in a

forsaken Depression mining town in West Virginia,
Demby wrote *Beetlecreek* in Italy and published the
novel three years after leaving Fisk. The novel is related
in the third person from the point of view of four characters, each of whom is struggling to extricate himself from
the death grip the community symbolizes. The story deals
primarily with Johnny Johnson, a fourteen-year-old boy
who has traveled to Beetlecreek to stay with his aunt and
uncle, while his widowed mother remains behind in a
Pittsburgh hospital. Johnny, feeling lonely and unloved,
befriends a white hermit named Bill Trapp, who lives on a
ramshackle farm on the edge of Beetlecreek. In order to
win the good opinion of a gang of boys his own age—the
Nightriders—Johnny ultimately betrays Bill, whom the
townsfolk unjustly have come to denounce as a pervert.

Bill is an enigmatic creature, whose presence in Beetlecreek has seldom disturbed the general torpor of the
community. But after fifteen years of self-imposed silence,
he determines to communicate and love the world, mainly
through Johnny. In the beginning he enjoys some success,
but he is finally met with suspicion and fear and he re-
treats once more to his solitude. Alternately imagined in
Johnny's dreams and fantasies as a saint and a shepherd,
he becomes something of a martyr when Johnny, suc-
cumbing to the deathlike atmosphere of Beetlecreek, turns
on him and attempts to burn down his house.

Interwoven with Johnny's relationship to Bill are accounts of David and Mary Diggs. David, Johnny's uncle,
represents a somewhat older version of his nephew. He,
too, as the novel opens, feels alienated and alone, but has
come to accept the passive drift of his life. He is awakened momentarily by his friendship with Bill, whom he
has met through Johnny. But when an old college sweet-
heart returns to town to attend a funeral, David forsakes
Bill and decides to run away with her. In so doing, David
pursues an illusion. Edith is a death figure, having been
hardened and corrupted in the big-city Negro ghettos.

Mary, David's wife, is the least defined of Demby's

characters. Her vitality has been drained by a loveless marriage and the stifling environment of Beetlecreek; her principal spiritual resources are the odd tidbits of gossip she gathers in the kitchen of the white folks she works for, and a driving ambition to become president of the Woman's Missionary Guild of her local church. Ironically, though, her success in gaining the latter is attended by the desertion of her husband and the murderous arson of her nephew, Johnny.

Thus *Beetlecreek* is a novel of defeat and death. Beetlecreek is itself a metaphor of death, a dreary and sluggish town whose inhabitants have lost all desire for change or hope for improved circumstances. Even its name suggests an arrested form of the evolutionary processes. Demby describes the creek itself thus:

> [David] would watch floating things—boxes, tin cans, bottles. He would watch how some of these things became trapped in the reeds alongside the shore. First there was a whirlpool to entice the floating object, then a slow-flowing pool, and, finally, the deadly mud backwater in the reeds. In the reeds would be other objects already trapped.

Demby employs a kind of stark, refined realism to seize his effects—not unlike some film directors who focus on seemingly prosaic objects in order to register a meaning that might otherwise be overlooked. Johnny, standing on the swinging bridge that spans the creek, observes, in the course of a conversation with some of the gang members, "a hole in the bottom plank of the bridge and in it was a waxy beetle struggling to get off its back." Demby depends more on closely realized visual elements than most novelists. The physical atmosphere of Beetlecreek informs the moral and spiritual dilemma of Demby's characters as much as anything they say or do. Thus Demby will focus on the light that falls over the town at certain hours of the day, or the wind-swept leaves and candy wrappers as they scatter along an empty street, or the freakishly warm weather of an Indian summer night. "The sky was a funny lavender color and always without a single cloud. There was a shimmery electric feeling in the air as if the world were enclosed in one neon tube."

Sometimes these images will become more obvious, as when Nature appears to suggest portents that hover ominously beyond the horizon. Indian summer weather lingers on well into autumn, out-of-season earthworms surface to the ground, birds swoop around the roofs and chimneys of houses as if "undecided what to do"—just as, in a fashion, Johnny and David remain suspended in moral indecision regarding what actions they will take concerning Bill Trapp, whether indeed they will save or betray him.

On an even more specific level, Demby will set a critical scene in a junk yard or cemetery, or he will describe a hearse as "shiny and low-slung like a super enameled beetle," or Bill Trapp's fingers "moving back and forth slowly like the antennae of insects." But these literal images are only part of the effect. The impact of the novel lies generally in the contrast between the vaguely looming violence that hangs over the town and the callowness of the townsfolk, the triteness of their talk, the superficiality of their behavior, the narrowness of their vision. In effect, Demby is saying that by the inert and passive qualities of their lives, they have chosen (by not choosing) evil for good, death for life, as revealed by the very essence of the physical atmosphere that engulfs them.

The images convey far more of the message of the novel than the dialogue. The sentences the characters utter are tired, flat and prosaic—as if the very act of expression were a spiritually exhausting experience. What the reader remembers best are scenes where scarcely any words are spoken: Bill Trapp staring silently at himself in the mirror, Mary alone and sobbing softly in the dark of her bedroom, Leader (the gang chief of the Nightriders) twirling a pigeon about by the neck until its head is torn from its body, Johnny racing noiselessly through the woods gripping two cans of gasoline to burn down Bill

Trapp's house. Demby shifts his scenes back and forth dramatically among his characters, viewing them, analyzing them at simultaneous moments wherever they may be. At the very moment Johnny is setting Bill's house afire, Mary is happily selling ginger cakes at the church fair, while David sits tensely on a bus-station bench preparing for his flight from Beetlecreek with Edith.

Although *Beetlecreek* is by no means a "Negro novel" in any provincial sense, its existential themes are particularly applicable to the Negro experience. The stifling and frequently destructive atmosphere of the ghetto has been portrayed many times by Negro authors, but here it is shown more as a kind of human condition than as a symptom of a specific social dysfunction. Moreover, such an atmosphere must intensify those universal existential feelings of dread and despair and terror that sociologists relate as being particularly prevalent among Negro slum dwellers. Demby himself recognizes as much when he represents David's thoughts of "how Negro life was a fishnet, a mosquito net, lace, wrapped round and round, each thread a pain. . . ." The nice little paradox of Demby's novel, however, is that this view of Negro life is not particularly Negro. The white man, Bill Trapp (the name is significant), is as much a Negro as the others—a pariah, an outcast, all his life he has known shame and fear and self-contempt. And the circle becomes complete when the Negro community persecutes him *because he is a white man*. Thus Negro life in all its deathly aspects is the mirror image of white society. Is it any wonder Demby chose to leave America?

Demby's second book, *The Catacombs*, published fifteen years later, is about a novelist named William Demby living in Rome, who is writing a novel about a Negro girl named Doris, who, when the novel opens, plays the role of one of Cleopatra's handmaidens in a film being made in Rome starring Elizabeth Taylor and Richard Burton. Doris is the daughter of one of Bill's old college sweethearts back in the States—and she has called on Demby, an established Rome resident, at the suggestion of her mother. Demby has introduced her to an Italian count with whom she proceeds to have an affair for the next two years. Doris sees Bill frequently and gives an account of herself which Demby will presumably incorporate in the novel.

In the course of her affair with the Count (who is married but living apart from his wife), she takes Bill as an occasional lover (also married but living with his Italian wife and son in a chic apartment), and at one juncture in the novel, she does not know whether Bill or the Count is the father of the baby to whom she is about to give birth. Doris determines the child is the Count's, but the baby is born dead (or does she lose it by abortion or miscarriage?—Demby leaves the question open), and the Count subsequently informs her that the British airline company he works for is transferring him to Hong Kong. Finally, Demby himself prepares to leave for New York, where he has been offered a position in an advertising agency. In the final passages of the book, the Count has taken Doris on a tour through the Catacombs, Rome's ancient cemetery for Christian martyrs. He loses her in the gloom, and as he pursues her along the maze of cold, dark corridors, calling out her name, the novel abruptly ends.

For Demby, plot in the conventional sense is an artifice that conceals the realities he endeavors to express. The fortunes of no one person can be isolated from any other's—indeed, all of existence, animate and inanimate, bears on the essential realities of the individual portrayed; hence any attempt to project the true life of a character in a novel must attempt to project at the same time the multifaceted elements of existence that constitute that life.

> What I mean, though, is simply this. That everything and everybody, real or invented, characters in books or in newspapers, the "news" itself, stones and broken bottles *do* matter, *are* important, if only they are looked at, if only

they are observed, just because they are composed of matter. Because everything and everybody, real or invented,
characters in books, even the books themselves, even the
book jacket and the colored ink on the cover design, is
composed of matter and for this reason matters, must
therefore breathe in harmony with a single governing law,
respond according to its aliveness, its *alertness*, to the degree that it is awake or awakened, to the shifting humors
of the wind-tormented involucre of our physical environment, which through Penelope's law of tapestry, Penelope's law of changeless change, can, as so often it does,
become transmuted into climate and weather, weather
peaceful or calm, these wild pregnant storm signals that
flash ignored through our minds. . . .

Moreover, the billions of years of accumulated time
create a pool of being on which all life acts, reacts and
interacts. The business of the novelist is to weave together
as many of these elements as he can. Demby construes
time-existence as being cyclic—as revealed in the cycle of
the seasons, as expressed in the death and resurrection of
Christ on the Christian calendar, as imagined in the periodic eclipses of the sun, and as symbolized by the two-
headed god Janus whose month January looks both
backward on death (winter) and forward to renewed life
(spring, Easter).

In order to reinforce what Demby here describes as
"illusory motion, the dreamlike sense of progression and
progress," images, events, colors, puns, patterns of
speech, dreams, and mythological, literary, and historical
allusions reappear in startlingly different contexts, as the
characters proceed along their way—themselves experiencing spiritual death and rebirth. As in *Beetlecreek*,
death as opposed to life is related to will-lessness, a failure of courage to act and to love. Its manifestations are
violence and nonfeeling. (It is interesting to note, in this
respect, that like the loveless David and Mary in *Beetlecreek*, the Count and his wife are unable to produce children.) Life and death are thus locked in immemorial
struggle as are good and evil in individuals.

Demby frankly discusses the rationale of the methods he will employ in the course of the book.

> When I began this novel, I secretly decided that, though I would exercise a strict selection of the facts to write down, be they "fictional" facts or "true" facts taken from newspapers or directly observed events from my own life, once I had written something down I would neither edit nor censor it (myself). . . . Novels, in theory, anyway, are supposed to be slices of life, slices of plum cake. So once the cook has created and stirred up the mixture, he has no moral right or obligation to censor, or select.

Just prior to this statement, Demby reproduces an introduction he had written for the sculptor, Losavio, at one of his exhibitions.

> Inanimate objects, be they tables or chairs, typewriters or pillows, Michelangelo's "Pietà," are formed of invisible universes of matter and energy: in this sense they are alive. Enclosed in a room, church or museum, house or castle, they influence one another—condition one another's existence in a house or in a castle.

And further on he describes the intellectual as one engaged in the "new warfare of ideas" and quotes approvingly from an editorial in an Italian newspaper that it is a war "fought in the name of peace. . . . There are no dead but the death of the animus of the people, of the nation. . . ."

Demby's methods of warfare are at first mystifying, but it is warfare directed not against the reader, but against evil. The key to Demby's tactics may be found on the opening pages of the novel. It is morning and he is in his studio awaiting Doris, who will tell him about her night with the Count. The sun shines on his Rotella collages "that have begun to dance like gorgeous jungle flowers." Before Doris arrives, he will read from a number of newspapers that lie on his desk.

From here on in the novel achieves something of a collage effect in which at odd moments the newspaper accounts Demby reads and quotes superimpose themselves, however precariously, on the narrative—the effect is a hovering sense of world and time on even the most private situations. But the various strands of the novel crisscross in other places as well. Demby may intrude on his story with seemingly vagrant thoughts of his own, with a letter someone is writing, with a street scene being played far outside the main arena of the drama by persons whom the reader does not know—or more frequently he may break into any dramatic action of his principals by projecting what some of the other major or minor characters may be doing or thinking at the precise moment. This simultaneity of presentation is presumably what Demby means when he speaks somewhere of "cubistic time." It is something almost animate—"time, always time, listening always listening, billions of years of imprisoned memory undistilled, electric-pointed stylus, plastic ballpoint pen." Actually, although the narrative generally unfolds in chronological order, Demby will, on occasion, shuttle back and forth in time in personal recollection or fantasy, or in a kind of Jungian race memory in which some odd newspaper item or disparate event suddenly assumes symbolic or archetypal importance. And yet the fragments do piece together. The novel begins and ends at the Easter season, and themes of death and resurrection become everywhere apparent like spirals within spirals.

If Demby's technique makes *The Catacombs* sound like something of a jigsaw, it is surprising to discover what intensely good reading the novel is. Part of the reason is Demby himself, around whom all the threads of the novel are bound. The prose is informed by a passion and honesty wherein the author tries to come to grips with himself in a world wracked by violence and stress. His principal means are his two "imaginary" or fictional characters, Doris and the Count, whose life-and-death confrontation is a reflection of Demby's own inward spiritual struggle. (Real-life characters stalk in and out of this novel as well—among them Demby's wife and son.) The Count,

for all his sophistication and elegance, is a death figure.
Centuries of inbreeding have left him spiritually debili-
tated. He endeavors unsuccessfully to reach out of himself, to act toward Doris according to his feelings, but his
entire conditioning inhibits him. For social reasons he is
afraid to bring Doris with him to Hong Kong, and it is
significant that the beginning and end of their relationship
takes place in a restaurant near the Catacombs. In contrast to the will-less Count, Demby poses another aristo-
crat he had once regarded as "dehydrated" who, as a
journalist, defied the threats of French Algerian terrorists
and remained in North Africa to record the terrible struggle for freedom. Thus Demby is saying that by an act of
will, of courage, it would not have been impossible for the
Count to transform himself had he so desired.

If the Count represents one segment of Demby's nature, Doris represents another. When the reader first
meets her, she is all energy and life.

> Doris burst into the room like an explosion of sunflow-
> ers. As always, her astonishing night-club-dancing vitality
> intimidates me. Always during these unpredictable visits of
> hers to my studio I become almost ashamed to be a writer.
> In her stormy fresh-minted presence, my soul shrivels and
> becomes clerklike and shabby. My writer's mask slips
> down over my neck and the grimly smiling skull of a
> certified accountant is revealed.

Later Demby says there is something about her that suggests fertility. She insists on wearing publicly her camera
make-up for the filming of *Cleopatra* and "her hairdo,
too, is authentically ancient Egyptian—a back-leaning
cone which somehow makes me think of a black lac-
quered cone of spider webs, a magical fertility symbol
floating detachedly over the masklike beauty of her en-
chanted nut-brown monkey face. . . ." Throughout the
course of the novel, Doris stands opposed to the Count as
a kind of life force. When she tells him she is going to
have his baby, he is angry and terrified at the prospect.

What is perhaps most interesting about Doris is that

her creative energies become intimately associated with her Negroness, her African ancestry. Demby speaks of her "forest-tapered legs," her "dream-secret Negro laughter." Beyond that, her négritude begins to assume a kind of saintly quality. She reminds the Count at their first meeting of "gold and rubies, of black Byzantine madonnas, amulets and incensed prayers." The Count's sister, a nun who has returned from the Congo, says that Africa is an "idea," a dream, where people still speak a "human language that the rest of humanity has forgotten," and that if society is to survive, it will have to become like Africa again and face "the realities of the tom-tom bed, the subtle clucking of the Bantu tongue." The Count himself admits to his wife that embracing Doris is like embracing "a girl in a dream."

Doris's symbolism is further enhanced by her Christlike sufferings. She accuses both Demby and the Count of being vampires; in drawing their sustenance from her, they suggest in involuted fashion worshippers at Communion. Doris's plight is made symbolic of the plight of all women who are used and suffer (and die) that their men might survive. On one occasion she mockingly proposes to Demby an apocryphal religion founded on Marilyn Monroe, whose suicide, she declares, was not unlike Christ's. She dreams of finding stolen silverware (a grail image) on Marilyn Monroe's grave, and the newspapers record a host of deaths by women who have taken their own lives after the example of the movie star. But it is clear that Demby intends his Christian symbolism mainly for Doris. He likens her afterward to Mary, Queen of Scots, and her disappearance in the Catacombs suggests the death of another Christian martyr.

Yet Doris and the Count, for all their symbolic status, ring true as people. Doris talks and sounds like a slightly worldly, slightly exuberant American college girl who pretends to brook no sentimentality.

> Oh, these Italians! These Italian men! I tell you, no kidding, the world's going to the dogs! If they ever decide

to drop Big Daddy's bomb, it's all the fault of these Latin
lovers, it's all the fault of these Italian men . . . !

She manages to keep up her skeptical, vaguely amused fa-
çade throughout the novel—especially with the Count,
about whom she really entertains no illusions. The Count,
for his part, always maintains his aristocratic demeanor,
despite the fact that he has lost some of his social relevance in bourgeois Italy. His speech is always polished,
his manners impeccable, and he remembers his ancestors.
His most passionate love scenes with Doris and his wife
are marked by an air of restraint, and it is clear that the
Count fears his emotions as much as he fears for his
position.

Demby casts his characters in remarkably real settings
—cafés, clubs, barbershops, beaches, drawing rooms,
country estates. As in *Beetlecreek*—but now with greater
skill—he focuses his camera on the seemingly irrelevant
to provide an authenticity that might not otherwise be
caught. A waiter, for example, staring glumly at a fly on
Doris's shoulder, suggests more about the atmosphere of
the café than a host of details. Demby cuts swiftly, im-
pressionistically, in and out from one scene to the next,
back to the brooding Demby who is imagining his novel—
catching his characters in unguarded moments, infusing
an air of reality into the dreamlike fragments of the structure.

It is a long way from the Beetlecreek of the Depression
era to Europe in the 1960's, but in some respects the
distance is not so great. For Doris and Demby, the entire
West begins to assume the character of a Beetlecreek
deathtrap. As Demby reads his day-to-day newspaper accounts of Algerian terrorists, murders, assassinations,
earthquakes, and other kinds of violence, he likens his
time to the Plague Year, the Ice Age, or those occasions
when the greed-ridden paladins and Knights Templar
wrought death and destruction in the wake of their con-
quests. The degradation of Europe is imaged in terms
reminiscent of the primeval ooze and slime of Beetle-

creek. The levels to which life has now descended are fishy and reptilian, and Demby introduces these metaphors unobtrusively. Fascist toughs who lurk around the entrance of a Spanish Civil War rally are suggestive of "catfish waiting to be sucked in a sewer." The paving stones on the Appian Way begin to bloom through a finely "tinseled drizzle like a disorderly array of unhatched dinosaur eggs." Newspapers report the appearance of sinister sea monsters off the coast of Calabria. An affluent South American lady keeps an iguana, "a miniature dinosaur," as a pet. The Spanish Civil War was "that *other* hour when the slimy dinosaur raised its head out of the stagnant, stinking pond." And the dreary primeval landscape of a Newfoundland airport awakens in Demby "thoughts of dinosaurs, of over-confident civilizations sinking beneath the slime."

There is, in addition, a considerable graveyard imagery. Demby attends the funerals of the Pope and of close friends and relatives, and observes on television the stiff, unreal ceremonies following the death of the American President. Rome and Greece, the foundation stones of Western civilization, are now viewed as cemeteries. The Count's wife, who has returned from a holiday in Greece, tells him:

> *Our* civilization, Raffaele—it didn't make sense to me. . . . Those lizards racing over the dead white marble like motorboats! I hated Greece! Something is wrong! . . . I went to Ephesus. The new Pope calls himself Paul. I wonder if he has ever been to Ephesus. What struck me most was the poverty. There were no trees. I became afraid of the sun. I hated that sinister purple sea. I felt like a tourist. I am sure the marble temples were a kind of joke. Built to fall.

And Doris, on their first meeting, tells the Count, "Rome is beginning to give me the creeps, all this antiquity, all this piling up dead things and dead people on top of each other. . . ."

But if the West is a graveyard, there remains the expec-

tation of rebirth. Although death images predominate,
there are hints of resurrection. A new Pope is elected and
makes a pilgrimage to Palestine, the birthplace of Christ.
There is even some hope that the Count's flight to the
East may rehabilitate him. Demby himself, secure now in
his faith, in the sanctity of all existence, decides to fly
back to the United States on Easter Monday. In a
semimock prophecy, he dreams of what New York will be
like.

> From their underground resting pace the restless ghosts
> of the swindled Iroquois and the Dutch swindlers will
> breathe Central Park's sweeter deeper green. It will be
> April in New York, flowers will bloom like tiny girl col-
> lege students in the forgotten cemeteries of Trinity Church
> and the Church of the Intercession. The cranky can-
> tankerous Lexington Avenue subway will suddenly run on
> time. I will sit at a desk in my skyscraper office, I will
> work to the rhythm of the Easter-Parade resurrected city.
> Smoothly but with green swiftness will flow the deep rivers
> that hold Manhattan in their sexually awakened maternal
> embrace. The season here in Rome grows late.

But for all his fond hopes, Demby is aware that the life-
and-death struggle will persist, and that troubled days lie
ahead. His is an almost Manichaean vision of being and
nonbeing locked in timeless combat, and the shifting fortunes of the combatants fluctuate like the ebb and flow of
the tides. Within this eternal pattern, it is the business of
men to assert their life forces so that the battle may not be
lost. And it is especially in America that the battle has
been very nearly lost. He tells Doris about an earlier visit
to America, where the raw hatreds and underground
tremors of social and racial violence portended for him
the conquest of Death.

Yet Demby in the novel returns to America a fulfilled
man. In part, of course, his deeply religious outlook has
discovered for him the role he plays in the cosmos. But in
part too, by means of his Christianity, he has recovered
his identity as a black man. For Doris has provided him

with the example of Christian martyrdom. And it is Africa, lush, green, and fertile, that gives him the sense of
Christian life. As the nun, the Count's sister, has put it,
here lies the source and redemption of the human race. In
contrast, Europe, white, cold, and sterile, has all but exhausted its spirit.

> Oh, God, Our Father, who is in Heaven, it is cold, it is
> cold, the white (European) world is cold, the flowers of
> narcissus bloom in the Himalayan Alps (When will the
> marguerite bloom). Oh, God, Our Father, who is in
> Heaven, it is cold, it is cold, the white (European) world
> is cold; cold the silly refrigerating thrill of cocaine, warm
> the God-ordained pillow of snow. Cool the color of
> money, crisp the rag-contented paper, warm to the touch.
> Technicians: wear white gloves that *pure* uranium and
> graphite (also waiters and maids) remain uncontaminated
> by human heat and sweat. Our Father, who is in Heaven, I
> am ashamed: white is not purity, contact lenses though
> they be tinted celestial do not necessarily make a saint.
> Hungrily we stick out our tongues (snowflakes cannot be
> hoarded nor placed on exhibition though each is a cameo
> of perfection). Oh, it is cold, the Caucasian world is
> cold. . . .

Demby's resolution is a very private one, as any spiritual conversion must be. Yet there is something beyond
the privacy of his vision that makes this book so striking.
Demby is one of those rare Negro Americans, immersed
in the culture of the West, who has discovered himself at
home in a civilization that has deeply wounded him. His
acceptance of the West has not negated his Negro identity
but has enhanced it.

And here lies the best—and only—hope for the future.
For if America is to survive and the races are to live in
peace, the Negro can neither be rejected nor integrated
out of existence, but must instead proudly take his place
in the sun as a black man, to enrich and reinvigorate a
civilization now sadly deficient in its best traditions.

Chapter X

Prospects: LeRoi Jones?

It is fashionable for studies such as this to conclude with a neat summary of definitions. And there is much to be said about common characteristics in the works of Negro authors. Protest, however artfully disguised, is always implicit. A bond of awakening nationalism runs through the works of all these writers, and themes of anger, frustration, and despair are everywhere apparent. Violence, in one form or another, latent or overt, is almost always expressed, and it is directed as much toward Negroes as whites. By and large there is an absence of humor. Heterosexual and romantic love is treated almost peripherally. And while a considerable weakness of Negro authors appears still to stem from their

190

ambivalent attitudes toward themselves and their environment, they remain the last dreamers of the American dream of freedom and equality.

But the whole range of pain and pride may be summed up in what Ellison has described as *invisibility*. For in demanding respect for his humanity, the Negro artist begins to respect himself. Or perhaps it is the other way around. In probing the deepest recesses of himself, he discovers the mysteries of his humanity, and the demand for recognition follows naturally. The point, of course, is that he is succeeding in what he has set out to do, and he has thereby won a place for himself in American letters.

There must be no condescension here. The successes and failures of these writers have been the successes and failures of American writing generally, and there have been no more significant recent works in American literature than some of those described in this book. Which brings us to the central paradox. Even while entering "the mainstream of American letters," the Negro writer has stepped back and asked himself Baldwin's question: "Do I want to be integrated into a burning house?"

But one wonders if this is not another mainstream. Are not white writers asking themselves the same question? And doesn't this put the Negro writer in the avant-garde rather than the rear guard? Even Ellison, who makes so much of his place in American life, cannot resolve his relationship to America aesthetically. Possibly this is because, as he suggests, so much of what we believe to be American life and history is illusory. Can the Negro artist construct a house of literature on these shifting sands? And yet that house is being built on a Negro experience hitherto closed to most white readers. Again one wonders, may this not be the underground experience of all Americans? As Ellison has asked: "Who knows, but that on the lower frequencies, I speak for you?"

One wants to say what is rarely said: that Negro writing, despite certain common characteristics, possesses a wide range and diversity of subject matter, style, theme, and attitudes. What remains to be said is that there are hosts of writers since the 1930's whose works command both a technical proficiency and a freshness of outlook. A number of them deserve more than honorable mention, and if they have been bypassed here, it is largely because we have attempted to encompass as wide a range of cultural attitudes as possible. It must suffice to state who some of these writers are: Ann Petry, Owen Dodson, John A. Williams, William Melvin Kelly, Carlene Hatcher Polite, Charles Wright, Kristin Hunter, and Paule Marshall; there are the poets—Margaret Walker, Gwendolyn Brooks, Robert Hayden, and Melvin Tolson; there are the playwrights—Theodore Ward, Lorraine Hansberry, and Lofton Mitchell. Nor should one overlook the autobiographers: Saunders Redding, Horace Cayton, and most recently Claude Brown. Richard Wright's autobiography, *Black Boy*, stands apart by itself as a classic of its kind.

What are the prospects? The Negro author is not likely to retire again into invisibility, or to settle for anything less than full expression in art, as in other areas of his experience. The air of apology is gone, and even the desire to be read and "understood" by white readers is no longer of special concern, but in certain respects the future of Negro writing still depends as much on white readers as on black. Articulation and communication require a common American response, and if there is only qualified recognition of the artist's voice, he may turn inward upon himself so as to defy comprehension, or outward upon the world so as to create only violence.

Perhaps the best illustration of such a possibility is the poet-playwright LeRoi Jones, who in the first half of the 1960's has transformed himself from a serious artist to a fiercely active nationalist, using his literary talents to effect what he regards as revolutionary ends. One may laud or deplore his motives, depending on one's point of view, but the fact is that much of Jones's recent writing has lost its depth and sensitivity while as propaganda it fails to arouse the violence Jones urges because, ironically, it is too erudite and subjective.

Jones, whose father was a postman, was born in Newark in 1934. He attended a mostly white high school in Newark and subsequently studied at Howard, Columbia, and the New School for Social Research. He served for a while in the Air Force, which carried him to Puerto Rico, Europe, Africa, and the Middle East. Jones's professional career has centered in and around New York's Lower East Side, Greenwich Village, Harlem, and Newark, and although he now eschews and excoriates "establishment" institutions, he has, in the course of his career, accepted the John Hay Whitney and Guggenheim awards to further his writing endeavors. He has also taught at the New School for Social Research and published in such "respectable" periodicals as *Poetry, Saturday Review,* and *The Nation.* In addition he has written jazz pieces for *Downbeat, Metronome,* and *The Jazz Review.*

It is probably a comment on our times that as Jones's works have deteriorated, he has been attracting more notoriety. Some of his first poems, collected in *Preface to a Twenty Volume Suicide Note* (1961), are hipster-zestful, irreverent but often sensitive, introspective and melancholy as well.

> Tonight, one star.
> eye of the dragon.
> 　　　　　The Void
> signaling.
> Reminding someone
> it's still there.

Although the element of rage is never too distant, he is capable of making it serve satiric ends. For example, having quoted Rimbaud's "Vous êtes de faux Négres," he writes after the manner of Eliot:

> O,
> these wild trees
> will make charming wicker baskets,

the young woman
the young black woman
the young black beautiful woman
said.
> These wild-assed trees
> will make charming
> wicker baskets.

(now, I'm putting words in her mouth . . . tch)

1

All afternoon
we watched the cranes
humping each other
> dropped
> our shadows
> onto the beach
and covered them over with sand.

. . . .

> I wobble out to
> the edge of the water

give my horny yell
& 24 elephants
stomp out of the subway
with consecrated hardons.

In recent years, Jones's anger has extended itself beyond his ability (or desire) to shape it artistically, and as
a result his plays and poems have lost themselves in a
kind of fretful hysteria. One suspects, however, that from
the beginning Jones has mistrusted poetry, possibly hated
it (as an expression of white civilization), and that he has
devoted his career to purging himself of his poetic sensibilities. Self-hate and self-destruction appear ironically in
the titles of some of his works: *Suicide Note, The Dead
Lecturer, The System of Dante's Hell.* Even his poetic
style is a destruction of syntax, order, and sense—as if
somehow to write may be an expression of hostility. In

The Dead Lecturer (1964), "Black Dada Nihilismus" is itself dadaist nihilist verse.

> A cult of death,
>
> need of the simple striking arm under
> the streetlamp. The cutters, from under
> their rented earth. Come up, black dada
>
> nihilismus. Rape the white girls. Rape
> their fathers. Cut the mothers' throats.
> Black dada nihilismus, choke my friends
>
> in their bedrooms with their drinks spilling
> and restless for tilting hips or dark liver
> lips sucking splinters from the master's thigh.
>
> Black scream
> and chant, scream,
> and dull, un
> earthly
>
> hollering Dada, bilious
> what ugliness, learned
> in the dome, colored holy
> shit . . .

What was once a source of strength, an energizing force in Jones's poetry—his rage, his contempt—has lately become a monomaniacal obsession, and his recent poems are fragments of fantasy, feeling, and ideas tossed together in a whirlpool of hysteria.

Some of his plays reveal the same centrifugal tendencies. *The Baptism*, produced on the Writers Stage in 1964, is unimaginably bad. Presumably an allegory (with characters called Minister, Homosexual, Boy, Woman) in "shocking" hip dialogue, the play attacks the prurience of American churches and American women. And although there are several corpses strewn about the stage as the curtain falls, the play fails of any movement whatsoever.

An equally bad play is *The Slave,* produced off Broadway in the same year. Here Jones imagines a future race war in which the leader of the blacks, a onetime poet, appears suddenly in the home of his white former wife, now respectably remarried, and threatens to take away the children, over whom she still has custody. (Jones in fact has two children by his white wife.) There is considerable frenzied gun-rattling, and many expletives and insults (mainly impugning the virility of white American males, white American culture, etc.) on the part of the poet-general. But there is little real action and little sense —and the audience gets the uneasy feeling that it has been made privy to an adolescent fantasy.

The Toilet, which was produced on the same program, is superior to *The Slave,* but it is hardly more than a theatrical exercise. In a sordid men's room in a slum high school, a number of Negro boys plot in raw obscenities to catch a white schoolmate who has sent one of them a love note. When Karolis is finally dragged in, bloody and semiconscious, he is made to fight with Foots, the boy to whom he addressed the note, and then with all the others, who pounce upon him and stomp him. After they all depart, leaving him lying dazed on the floor, Foots returns by himself, throws his arm about Karolis, and begins to weep. Jones does manage to suggest something of the nature of his characters as they move nervously across the stage, aligning themselves first with one and then with another of their comrades in brief senseless flareups, while awaiting the arrival of the white homosexual. He is not so successful with Karolis and Foots, but there is genuine pathos in the final revelation that the Negro does indeed love the white boy.

Jones's best play, and one that stands up rather well (he won an off-Broadway award for this), is *The Dutchman* (1964). The action takes place in a New York subway car, and deals with a white girl's verbal seduction-castration of a "respectable-looking" Negro boy. By outright insult, innuendo, and ridicule, she tears away any illusions he may have regarding his status and history in American life. When at last she calls him a woolly-headed Uncle Tom, he turns on her and pours out all the scorn and hatred he feels toward whites. At the end of his speech she knifes him. Some of the other passengers dispose of the corpse, and she scrawls some kind of notation in a notebook. Then, as the play ends, she begins to look seductively at another young middle-class Negro who has just entered the car. *The Dutchman* owes more than a little to Albee's *The Zoo Story*, but Jones holds his own. There is a smouldering tension to the exchange between the two principals—and the rhetoric is often first rate.

In addition to his plays and poems, Jones has produced three books.* The first of these, *Blues People* (1964), is an attempt to define the American Negro through his music. Jones is hard put throughout the work to isolate the unadulterated African and Negro elements in American blues and jazz, and the elaborate sociological conclusions he draws from his investigations appear somewhat disproportionate to the evidence he offers. On Jones's behalf, though, it must be said that he has researched his material carefully and, theories aside, has made a rather informative contribution to the literature of jazz.

Jones's other nonfiction work, *Home* (1967), is a collection of articles, essays, and reviews, in which the reader can, if he wishes, trace the development of Jones's political, literary, and social views as they become more and more militant and nationalistic. But since Jones here says nothing that Wright, Baldwin, and Malcolm X have not said better, it would be tedious to repeat what he does say. What may be interesting biographically is that Jones in this book (and at greater length in a lecture he once delivered at Berkeley) cites an incident at Howard when a dean castigated him for eating a watermelon on campus, thereby endangering Howard's public image of the edu-

---

* A fourth book, *Tales* (1967), was published too late for discussion here.

cated Negro. It was at Howard, Jones writes, that he was
shocked into realizing the "sickness" of the Negro—
which suggests that discovering racism at an age well past
the impressionable years may produce more extreme reac-
tions (Wright, Jones) than the racism others have experienced all their lives.

Jones's one novel, *The System of Dante's Hell* (1965),
deals mainly with the narrator's remembrances of his
adolescent years in Newark. The prose is largely in fragments and simple sentences, and the memories are associated without transition, as they would be in a dream or
nightmare. There is some attempt at traditional narrative
at the end, but the novel as a whole must be termed, for
want of a better word, "experimental." Despite Jones's
attempt to structure his hell ("the torture of being the
unseen object and the constantly observed subject") according to Dante's nine circles, the relationship is casual,
and the novel is as explosive and directionless as some of
Jones's poems. Yet the hell is very real. It is equally a song
of self-disgust and an act of hostility toward the reader.
"This thing, if you read it, will jam your face in my shit.
Now say something intelligent!" The narrator successfully
evokes the sordid, dreary sounds and images of Negro
slums, and there are fleeting glimpses of sexual experiences with males and females. But above all the novel
reads like a kind of melancholic obsessive return to the
past, as if Jones, not unlike Jean Toomer years before
him, were seeking "absolute pain," possibly to discover
himself at last, possibly to obliterate himself.

It would be an easy matter to dismiss Jones as a
maniacal racist, or (for some white readers, at least) passively and masochistically to accept all his mad pronouncements as great social truths. The fair-minded
reader must, of course, admit the value of some of Jones's
work, despite the hysterical nonsense Jones assumes to be
necessary to racial leadership. But the real tragedy of
Jones is not simply his loss to us (for the moment, in any

event) as an artist, but that Jones feels he has to submerge his humanity in order to find himself.

The despair of LeRoi Jones and those like him is of
course understandable. Whether or not they signal a
"trend" perhaps depends more on their America than on
themselves.

Bibliography

I. *Anthologies*

Brown, Sterling A., Arthur P. Davis, and Ulysses Lee, eds., *The Negro Caravan*, New York, 1941.

Calverton, Victor F., ed., *Anthology of American Negro Literature*. New York, 1929.

Hill, Herbert, ed., *Soon One Morning*. New York, 1963.

Locke, Alain Leroy, ed. *A Decade of Self Expression*. Charlottesville, Virginia, 1928.

————, ed., *The New Negro: An Interpretation*, New York, 1925.

Watkins, Sylvestre C., ed., *Anthology of American Negro Literature*. New York, 1944.

Williams, John A., ed., *The Angry Black*. New York, 1962

II. *Literary History and Criticism*

The American Negro Writer and His Roots: Selected Papers from the First Conference of Negro Writers, March 1959. New York, 1960.

Bone, Robert A., *The Negro Novel in America*. New Haven, 1965.

Brown, Sterling A., *The Negro in American Fiction*. Washington, D.C., 1937.

————, *Negro Poetry and Drama*. Washington, D.C., 1937.

Butcher, Margaret Just, *The Negro in American Culture*. New York, 1956.

Ford, Nick Aaron, *The Contemporary Negro Novel*. Boston, 1936.

Gloster, Hugh Morris, *Negro Voices in American Fiction*. Chapel Hill, N.C., 1948.

Gross, Seymour L. and John Hardy, eds., *Images of the Negro in American Literature*. Chicago, 1966.

Hill, Herbert, ed., *Anger, and Beyond: The Negro Writer in the United States*. New York, 1966.

Hughes, Carl Milton, *The Negro Novelist*. New York, 1953.

Littlejohn, David, *Black on White: A Critical Survey of Writing by American Negroes*. New York, 1966.

Loggins, Vernon, *The Negro Author: His Development in America*. New York, 1931.

Redding, J. Saunders, *To Make a Poet Black*. Chapel Hill, N.C., 1939.

Index